John Veitch

Knowing and Being

John Veitch

Knowing and Being

ISBN/EAN: 9783337219291

Printed in Europe, USA, Canada, Australia, Japan

Cover: Foto ©Thomas Meinert / pixelio.de

More available books at **www.hansebooks.com**

ESSAYS IN PHILOSOPHY

𝔉irst 𝔖eries

KNOWING AND BEING

KNOWING AND BEING

BY

JOHN VEITCH, LL.D.

PROFESSOR OF LOGIC AND RHETORIC IN THE
UNIVERSITY OF GLASGOW

WILLIAM BLACKWOOD AND SONS
EDINBURGH AND LONDON
MDCCCLXXXIX

PREFACE.

THE Essays in this volume were given as Lectures to the advanced class of Logic and Metaphysics in the University of Glasgow, during the present session, 1888-89. This class was instituted by me in 1867. The attendance on it is wholly voluntary; and, in the current session, its numbers, though not large, show an increase, notwithstanding the lack of appreciable encouragement to prosecute the higher departments of Philosophy in the University of Glasgow, or indeed in any Scottish University. I hope to be able to publish, in sequence, portions of the various courses of lectures originally delivered to this class, during the last twenty-two years. These will be to me a grateful memorial at least of hours spent with an audience of youths, fresh-hearted and full of hope, with the promise and the charm of life still before them, who have shown a real concern for the higher questions of Speculative Philosophy.

J. V.

THE UNIVERSITY, GLASGOW,
April 1889.

CONTENTS.

	PAGE
INTRODUCTORY, ...	1
I. RECENT THEORIES, ...	10
II. NATURE AND CONSCIOUSNESS, . .	35
III. REALITY, ...	84
IV. RELATION, ...	129
V. TRANSCENDENTAL DEDUCTION AND NATURE, .	161
VI. EXTERNAL PERCEPTION, . . .	178
VII. THE ETERNAL CONSCIOUSNESS, . .	232
VIII. THE INFINITE SELF-CONSCIOUSNESS—GENERAL CONSIDERATIONS—SUMMARY, .	269
IX. PHILOSOPHY OF RELIGION, . . .	301

KNOWING AND BEING.

INTRODUCTORY.

The problem of Philosophy may be said to be twofold: on one side is the question, What do we know? on the other, What is? Obviously the first question has its main interest for us as leading to the second. Our knowledge acquires interest and importance from what it teaches us regarding what is—regarding our own Self, the World, and God. Knowledge is a means, not an end. We do not know merely that we may contemplate or speculate. We know that we may believe. As knowledge issues in belief, it further issues in action, for we act as we believe.

I put the question as to Knowing first; for it seems to me irrational to put that of Being first, or to attempt to settle any question about Being

—about what is—first or apart from Knowing. That is a vain method, as seems to me, though it is professed, but always inconsistently acted upon.

Further, I put the question as to knowing not only first, but in this form — What do we know? In these times it will be found pretty frequently put as, What can we know? I have no objection to this form of the question. I think we must in the end come to it. We must consider the question as to the conditions, the reach, the limits of human knowledge. But I distinctly object to its being put first. And I find very great disadvantages arising from its being so put. The risk of giving it the first place is, that we are apt to lay down conditions regarding perhaps one part or sphere of our knowledge only; and when we have got those partial conditions or limitations, we set them up as the laws of all knowledge, and come thus to exclude from knowledge many things that we do know. Hence I distinctly object to what is called the Theory of Knowledge, if this be not preceded by a thorough examination and analysis of what we do as a matter of fact know in and by consciousness in all its forms,— from Sense-Perception, through Memory, Imagination, Thinking—including concepts, judgments, reasonings — up even to that side of our consciousness which is conversant with what we call the Infinite, the Absolute, the Unconditioned, the Divine. If, for example, we start simply with the knowledge we get in Sense-Perception, and draw out its conditions and laws, and then carry them all through our knowledge as its laws, we shall make the blunder of limiting knowledge to a single, and perhaps comparatively insignificant, portion of its sphere. The laws of our knowing the object in time and space are not necessarily the laws of our knowing all objects. Yet this has been actually done in philosophy; and it has been done through our setting up the question as to what we can know, before that as to what we do know. In a word, we must have Psychology —that is, a study of consciousness in its widest sphere—before we can have Metaphysics, or the science of reality; and we must further have psychology in all its fulness before we can have what is called the Theory of Knowledge, for the simple reason that you cannot give the theory of a thing before you know what the thing is, and is in all its completeness. The mistake in ancient philosophy was to begin metaphysics before psychology; the mistake, common enough in modern philosophy, is to begin the theory of knowledge before psychology, and before we have any means of knowing what we know, or knowing knowledge as a fact of experience.

In this connection there occurs to us the contrast between ancient and modern method—practically between Aristotle and Descartes. In ancient philosophy, especially the Aristotelic, there is obviously the prominence of the object in the method of investigation,—being as being, and the essential attributes of being as such; then a process downwards from this to its special forms: and although *being* does not appear as the *summum genus* of the categories of Aristotle, still it is there influentially. It is the objective forms, the forms of reality, as embodied chiefly in language, which determine the classification.[1] And it is the modes of real judgment—judgment about things—on which the logical forms in the *Organon* are based. But clearly those objective forms or facts cannot be considered apart. They are at first for us, as they are in knowledge; and knowing in every scheme of philosophy must come in for its share of attention and scrutiny. Things as they stand in relation to our acts of cognition —ultimately this is the point of view; not, however, taking them merely as they now stand in mature experience, but considering genesis, growth, increase of knowledge as well.

[1] Cf. *Institutes of Logic*, p. 51.

The modern point of view, that of Descartes, is generally spoken of as rather the analysis of knowing than the analysis of being, and in a good sense it is so. His *cogito ergo sum* has unquestionably its starting-point in consciousness, and he proceeds to being through consciousness. Moreover, he inculcates the doctrine that the mind is better known than the body or object; and he seeks to build up philosophy on the basis of clear and distinct ideas, and mainly by deduction. But it would be a mistake to suppose that in the method itself, or even as unfolded by Descartes, there is any exclusion of a regard to the object or varied objects of knowledge. Descartes certainly never tried to evolve knowledge out of the simple acts or operations of knowledge, divorced from the variety of objects in experience; nor did he set up knowing, as the instrument of philosophy, to the exclusion of known being. In the first principle of his philosophy—the immediate implication of self-being in self-consciousness,—there is ample recognition of being as known. The gulf supposed to exist between knowing and being is here at once bridged, for the being conscious in a given instance is the being for the time, and knowing and being are fused in one intellectual comprehension. Here subject is not divorced from object, but subject and object become implicative. And whatever may be thought of his tendency to exaggeration in deduction from the clearness and distinctness of the idea, and its fatal consequences in absorbing being in knowing, making belief simply a harmony of concepts, carried to an extremity in Spinoza,—there is both in the *Meditations* and the *Principles* a very ample recognition, in practice, of the need of studying mental operations in the light of their objects. Thinkers may imagine that they can study knowing to the exclusion of the variety in the objects known; they delude themselves. The acts of cognition not only cease to be various, and thus adequate to reality; they actually cease to be. The study of being out of knowing is vain; not less empty is the study of knowing apart from being.

It may be said that, on the whole, the view which puts the investigation of knowing before being has prevailed in modern philosophy, and it is only lately that any unfaithfulness to the method has been shown. It is even true that Psychology, as a rule, has gone before the Theory of Knowledge, though the psychological investigation has been hampered by hypotheses as to the supposed ability or inability of the mind to know in given spheres. It will be found that the various doctrines and theories of Sense-Perception have turned a good deal, for example, on the question as to whether anything can be perceived which is not a sensation or mode of the mind, or "idea" in the mind. All this proceeds, as seems to me, on a misapplication of the true method. We set out to seek knowledge, and we hamper ourselves by a system or hypothesis about knowledge, already formed or traditionally got, and thus we frustrate our own efforts.

It ought also to be kept in mind that "knowing" and "being" are abstractions. There is no knowing in our experience without a knower; there is no being realisable by us apart from something that actually is. Further, there is no knowing which is not a definite act of knowing — either perceiving, or remembering, or judging, or something else that is definite. Hence we cannot set up *knowing* as a thing to be inquired into in the first place. We can deal only with this or that act of knowledge, and deal with these in succession, until we have exhausted as to nature the possible acts of our knowledge. Thus, and thus only, can we set down the conditions—the essential conditions—of our knowing; those apart from which there is no object of knowledge; those apart from which there is not *this* or *that* act of knowing. Anything else is a mere abstraction, and a worthless abstraction, and its conditions are not the conditions of actual knowledge. In recent systems of philosophy, the whole of the true relations of these questions has been misconceived and perverted.

The same is true of the terms "Pure Being," "Consciousness," "Thought." Being, or pure being, is simply qualityless being—being not determined as *this* or *that*. There is nothing corresponding to such a conception in reality. Being must be related to some definite subject ere it can mean anything real or actual,—ere, indeed, we can properly realise it as meaning anything. Every object of thought, as thought, is regarded as existing or real, in the sense of its affirmation as an object of thought, whether it be the percept of a time object or the concept of that which may be at any time. Being is simply the abstraction or universalised concept of this fact. To be studied, being must be studied not *per se*, but in its varied applications to real things. But this application cannot come out of being *per se;* it must be helped or furnished from another source, a sphere beyond the limits of the abstraction. Pure being is simply an empty notion.

In the same way there is no reality corresponding to the term "Consciousness," or even to "a consciousness;" that is, there is nothing in reality convertible with it. There are conscious acts,—definite, individual, specific,—successive and coexisting in time. "Consciousness" represents their common element, abstracted by us, and raised into a concept. It is the element, so to speak, of knowledge, recognition, or "awareness" on our part of certain acts with definite contents. And we can put a meaning into "consciousness" by thinking it as exemplified in an apprehensive conscious act (real), or in a conceiving conscious act (ideal). But thus only has it reality. Far less is it a person or an actor. It ought not to be hypostatised, and made to do what alone something more, that is, a conscious subject, can do.

The same remarks apply to "Thought," which is an abstraction of precisely the same character and origin. It represents what is common to individual or definite acts of thought in different times; yet it is set up to do and to be what only that which grounds it—a thinker—can do or be.

KNOWING AND BEING.

I.—RECENT THEORIES.

THERE has grown up of late in our philosophical literature a mode of dealing with its questions, which has at least the merit of novelty—to say nothing of the mark of foreign importation. It is not quite to be identified with the teachings of the *Critique of the Pure Reason;* but it owes its origin in great measure to that treatise. The predominant doctrines of the *Critique* are reproduced in what may be called the new school, somewhat modified or transformed, it may be, in certain cases, but still essentially Kantian. The influence of Hegel is also visible: Hegel, indeed, has been read into Kant abroad, and also in this country, so as to correct him, supply his deficiencies, and carry him on to a higher stage of development. What Kant regarded as merely a form of knowing has been translated into a form of being. The subjective necessity has been transformed into the objective existence, and thought and reality identified. For lack of a better word it would not be improper to name the way of looking at things which results from this fusion of Kant and Hegel as Neo-Kantian.

We shall find, however, as we proceed, that this new system is not wholly of foreign importation. It borrows an essential principle from philosophy nearer home. It first of all lays one hand on that prime inspirer of modern thinking, alike in its destructive and in its constructive sides, David Hume; and stretching out the other to Kant, it seeks to fuse the two, to supplement *The Treatise of Human Nature* by the aid of the *Critique of the Pure Reason*, and so reproduce for us, or rather construct, the World, Man, and God. The principle underlying the whole of Hume's speculative reasoning, whether accepted traditionally or put forward as true, is the limitation of consciousness to perceptions, that is, impressions and ideas, or states of consciousness. Neither Kant himself nor the Neo-Kantians ever rise beyond this limitation. They do not, whether logically or not, regard Hume's impression *per se*, or apart from objective relation, as an object of knowledge; but they deny explicitly that any object, save a feeling or sensation, can be directly apprehended by us, or can come as an element into the complexus which constitutes an object of perception or even of knowledge. The nihilism of Hume, when his principles are fully carried out, is abundantly acknowledged and proclaimed. But this is to be counteracted by the new philosophy. It is for us to consider whether the correction borrowed from Kant is of avail; whether the method of constructing objects is a sound one, whether, in a word, the construction is or is not based on truth of fact; and whether, looking to basis and construction alike, there is truly and logically any advance to results beyond those reached by Hume himself. Possibly it may turn out that Neo-Kantianism is but Hume writ large.

The essential feature of the method of Neo-Kantianism, as appears to me, is its analysis of Knowing and its consequent determination of what is meant by Being; and, indeed, of Being itself. It practically accepts Kant's question as to how knowledge is possible; and it proceeds, either following Kant literally or with certain modifications, to lay down the essential conditions of knowledge, those conditions apart from which no object whatever is known—perceived or conceived. And it may, at least in certain prominent cases, be held as adopting Kant's method of determining those conditions—viz., that known as Transcendental Deduction, or the Transcendental Deduction of the Categories.

The analysis of Knowing necessarily affects the theory of Being. What are called the logical, properly metaphysical, conditions of knowledge, may be held to limit our knowledge of reality simply, with indefinite possibilities beyond; or they may be held as limiting Being or reality itself within their own extension. So that Being as known or knowable by us may be held to be the only Being. It may even be held that the most general, universal, or, properly, abstract conditions of knowledge by us—called categories—are, in an alleged concatenation, the universe of Being; so that from the analysis of what we call knowledge we may come to regard the laws we find as the true, inner, essential being of things—the world, man, and God. For once we set out on the path of abstraction, and look only at the conditions of the possibility of knowledge, the ascent is easy to the view that the most abstract formula which can represent those conditions is the ultimate conception of the universe and adequate to God Himself. If, for example, finite knowledge and being be identified with the conception of "relation," we have not far to go to make the highest in Knowing and Being a sum simply or centre of relations—a vast possibility of development through finite consciousness—and call it an Eternal or Universal or Infinite Consciousness.

The analysis of Knowing thus specially affects the three acknowledged forms or kinds of Being —viz., Nature, Self or Man, and God—and our views as to what these mean and are. The principal point here in reference, in the first place, to nature, is the change in the recognised view of it. When we say that we perceive or know what we call nature, or an outward world, the reality of a non-ego, we do not mean also that in so doing we make or constitute nature, that is, the facts and the order of those facts, which form its known contents. We quite plainly distinguish knowing and being in this instance. We hold as different the object perceived in the moment of perception; we distinguish it from mere feeling; and we hold the permanence and independence of existence, in some form or other, through and amid our changing perceptions and conceptions of what we call things.

But Neo-Kantianism changes all this for us. To know nature or the outward world, that is, to perceive and conceive it, is not merely to recognise it, it is truly to make or constitute it.

"The understanding makes nature," in a sense, no doubt, afterwards to be made more explicit; but substantially it is held that nature is made for us by what is called our "thought," or by "thought," for ultimately we are to find that "our thought" is not ours in the sense of exclusive or even personal possession, but a form of thought, or consciousness, designated Universal, Infinite, Eternal. Thought or consciousness, and in the first instance as possessed by us, is not only a perceiving or a conceiving of what has for itself a reality, but it is the very constitution of that reality. The dualism of nature and thought or intelligence is abolished; and we have in its room a thought-created or constituted nature or world of outward things. For the ordinary names are in each case retained, even after they have been eviscerated entirely of their recognised meaning.

When we come to the application of results to Man, Self, or Person, we find also a considerable change in the point of view, or meaning of the terms. Instead of a conscious subject as the one factor in knowledge, we usually hear of a "consciousness," or "thought," as doing the work of knowing and making. This is not a correct or justifiable use of words; it is a substitution of the act for the actor, of the knowing for the knower, even of the object of the knowledge for the knowing. But it indicates the bearing of the theory on our personality or self-hood; and this is simply a minimising of it in the first instance, for it is practically merging the self in its act; and from this the transition is easy to regard the act as one not of our personality or self at all, but either as complete in itself, or as that of a Single Supreme Consciousness, regarded as working in all, and called Infinite or Eternal. The use of terms in this instance is characteristic, and points to what may be called the *abstractionalism* which dominates the whole of Neo-Kantianism. When we call to mind that this novel theory is introduced chiefly for the purpose of founding a rational system of Ethics, as opposed to a natural one, and find it given as the only possible basis of a true moral theory, the incongruity and inaptitude of the lowering, even effacing, of personality stand out in strong relief. The method, of which this is but one example, will be fully illustrated in the sequel. It will be found to be the treatment of abstractions as if they were realities; and holding that to be true of reality which is true only of an abstraction, and, *e converso*, holding that to be false of reality which is not true of an abstraction.

We find very little reference in Neo-Kantianism to the knowledge of other selves in the world of our experience. We are accustomed to think that there are other people in the world — personalities like ourselves. The world of nature is not, to our thinking, the only non-ego. Each ego different from me is to me a non-ego, — in the strictest sense, a not-self to me. The very meaning of self-hood or personality points to an absolute mutual exclusion of the reality of each self. All egos lie out of each other: on this condition alone can they remain egos. How we come to know these, and to have the conviction that they are, is another question. It is a fact that we have the conviction; we certainly should be surprised to learn, as the conclusion of a philosophy, that "I" is in the world, but not "WE." Yet I do not find any fair or face-to-face treatment of this problem, or any definite conclusion about it. If, however, we are to apply the principle that conceiving an object also constitutes that object, that conceiving the world of nature makes it, how are we to escape extending the principle to the world of Selves, which we believe to be? Another self is not directly apprehended by us. We infer it only from certain appearances. But these appearances are "feelings," and they are created and constituted objects of knowledge by us. They have no transcendent existence, in time at least, apart from our mind. How, then, can the supposed or inferred self be an entity apart from our mind? The "feelings" through which it is known are in my mind; it itself, as an object of thought, can thus only be in my mind. How, then, is it different from me? How can it be another self? How is it less a creation of mine than what I call the world of outward nature? In that case, what precisely would be the kind of reality we should have to attribute to another self, or one said to be different from me the knower? And on what would its reality depend? All I find is, that the selves of the world are to be regarded as modes or forms, or something of this sort, of the Supreme Infinite Consciousness, of which I eventually discover myself to be a manifestation. Whatever other conclusion follows from this, it is quite clear that there cannot be any real difference, or difference fitted to constitute a self at all in the world, if every one is but the form or manifestation of one hidden self, deploying itself through all.

With regard to the third great point — the nature and reality of God — the highest question of ontology or metaphysics — the answer given by Neo-Kantianism follows the line of thought already indicated. It seeks gradually to work up, through certain processes of analysis, to what is called a Universal, or Infinite, or Eternal Self-consciousness, regarded as the Divine Self or God. This conception is a very marked instance of the fusion of Kantianism and Hegelianism. Kant, as is well known, finds what may be regarded as the ultimate condition of knowledge, and of at least phænomenal reality, in "the synthetic unity of apperception or consciousness," or the transcendental unity of self-consciousness. But while the process or act of synthetic unifying is needed, this does not, in Kant's view, imply a real self or ego at the root of it. The self here is nothing beyond a unifying process conceived as necessary to the constitution of knowledge ; and the unified product, the known world, is nothing unless as in relation to the self or process. This is the pure ego, but it is not realised in any actual self-consciousness. It is, in fact, a mere abstraction of the form of consciousness, or the most general statement of the condition of combination according to which we actually know or possibly can know. Now that which with Kant was a simple necessity of thought in constructing experience, becomes with the later thinkers a reality, and that which gives reality to the world of nature and man—being and knowledge. While Kant shrank from regarding the transcendental self as real, as more than a mere logical abstraction, and especially from identifying it with God, Neo-Kantians boldly make the advance, and hold the self to be real, and also to be God. In this they follow the spirit, if not the letter of Hegel, with whom reality or thought or categorising are identical. What is rational— that is, what is thought under certain categories— is real, and what is real is rational.[1] The transcendental self of Kant becomes the one side of a conception, of which the manifold of things or the world is the other. It is a principle of relation, or unifying, which cannot exist apart from the relation or relations which it is supposed to constitute. It is, in a word, the unity of the manifold, this unity being necessary to the manifold and the manifold to the unity.

Now, without meanwhile going fully into a discussion of this view of the Divine reality and of its grounds, it may at least be said that such a conception of Deity does not in any way fulfil what are usually regarded as the requirements of the conception. It is clear, in the first place, that the predicates of power or causality, of activity and act, cannot apply to such a subject. Indeed the conception of this self as the eternal unity of the one and the many, expressly excludes

---

[1] This point has been clearly and ably put by Professor Seth in his recent treatise, *Hegelianism and Personality*. See especially pp. 423-435.

them. It never existed in a state of potency or simple causality, and therefore never could manifest activity in any sense we can attach to the term. It is hence spoken of as an eternal act; but neither is it an act, for this is essentially a time conception, implying commencement and completion. It is not an eternal act; it is truly, if it is anything, an eternal *is*. And this is simply to identify it with the sum of being in the universe, and to say that this is two-sided, one and many, or one in many, and eternally so. Anything thus approaching even the idea of creation or creative power is utterly excluded, whatever sense we may attach to those words. To speak of it as having "a constitutive activity equivalent to creation" is a simple contradiction in terms. The eternity of the act completely excludes this, for this is equivalent to the eternity of the *is*. To raise this into an entity, and to endow it even with the attributes of *self* and *consciousness*, is simply to transfer to an abstraction, out of time, conceptions not implied in it, which it cannot yield or explain, and which, so applied, become absolutely meaningless. This at least is true, that the ideas of creation and creative energy are emptied of meaning, and for them is substituted the conception or fiction of an eternally related or double-sided world, not of what has been done, but of what always is. It is another form of the see-saw philosophy. The eternal self only is, if the eternal manifold is; the eternal manifold is, if the eternal self is. The one in being the other is or makes itself the one; the other in being the one is or makes itself the other. This may be called a unity; it is rather, if we might invent a term suited to the new and marvellous conception, what may be designated an unparalleled and unbegotten *twinity*. It will be for us to consider the processes of thought through which this conception is sought to be established. Perhaps it may be found that they are as little worthy of acceptance as the entity to which they are supposed to lead up, while they affect directly and injuriously true conceptions of the sphere of experience and finite reality generally. It will at least be a service to philosophy, and the truthfulness of the speculative habit, to require that terms no longer expressive of received meanings, but of others even subversive of the received, should not continue to be used as if they retained their present connotation.

Neo-Kantianism, as represented alike by Mr Green, M. Renouvier, M. Pillon, and others, is, as I have said, simply an attempt to fuse the phænomenalism, or rather impressionalism, of Hume, with what may be called the apriorism of Kant.

It is held that Hume was right in so far as he limited (presented) knowledge to impressions, or states of consciousness; he was wrong in so far as he did not include relation, necessary relations imposed on the impressions. Hume was right in concluding from the limitation of sense knowledge to impressions, that no idea could be formed of external objects distinct from the perception, and continuing to be after the perception ceased. But he did not fully recognise the place of relations or law in regulating those impressions. And he did not recognise the validity of the inference from me as a thinking subject, or rather sum of representations, to other thinking subjects or centres of representations, analogous to me. In these foreign centres of representations lies the true external world.[1]

The belief of mankind is that there are external objects which are distinct from our perceptions, and to which our perceptions are related as to their causes. This is a universal illusion, according to Hume,—this belief in objects *distinct* from our perceptions, and *continuous* even after the perception. Imagination gives a representative character to impressions, which belongs only to ideas. Imagination confounds likeness with identity. Similar impressions occur, or are pro-

[1] Cf. Pillon, *Psychologie de Hume*, Introduction, §§ x., xi.

duced, at different intervals; we unite these impressions in one and the same idea, suppressing the intervals, and adding to likeness of nature continuity of existence. The link of the similar impressions is supposed to be an external object, one and the same. The impressions thus become representations and effects of this object.[1]

" 'Tis universally allowed by philosophers, and is besides pretty obvious of itself," says Hume, "that nothing is ever really present with the mind, but its perceptions or impressions and ideas. . . . Now, since nothing is ever present to the mind but perceptions, and since all ideas are derived from something antecedently present to the mind; it follows that it is impossible for us so much as to conceive or to form an idea of anything specifically different from ideas and impressions. Let us fix our attention out of ourselves as much as possible: let us chase our imagination to the heavens, or to the utmost limits of the universe, we never really advance a step beyond ourselves, nor can conceive any kind of existence but those perceptions which have appeared in that narrow compass."[2] Again: "The only existences of which we are certain,

---

[1] Cf. Pillon, *Psychologie de Hume*, Introduction, § 9.
[2] Hume, *Treatise of Human Nature*, B. I. p. ii., § vi., p. 123 (ed. 1739).

are perceptions which, being immediately present to us by consciousness, command our strongest assent, and are the first foundation of all our conclusions."[1] This is the one grand premiss, as we shall see, of the whole of Neo-Kantianism. It borrows, no doubt, category, especially relation, from Kant, makes this its category of categories, and seeks thereby to lick sensations into shape, and so call them objects. But any other object, so far as the external world is concerned, it never gets than an aggregate of sensations, and it will be found in the sequel that it thus logically cuts itself off from all connection with, all knowledge either of other individual selves in the world, or of God, in any true sense of these terms.

Now, what precisely is the meaning of this statement of Hume? It may mean—

(1.) That if we apprehend or know an object, we consciously apprehend or know it, that consciousness is implied in the perception of the object.

This is a wholly indisputable statement, and in no way touches the question as to whether the object apprehended or known has or has not an existence distinct from the conscious act of knowing. Some objects, even, we may recognise as having their whole reality in and during the con-

---

[1] Hume, *Treatise of Human Nature*, B. I. p. iv., § ii., p. 370.

scious act, as, for example, a state of pain which passes away; others we may not be able to regard as so limited in their reality. They may be so distinct from the conscious act, that we are not able to say that they pass from reality when they pass from our knowledge. And thus the whole question as to the possibility and the nature of their supersensible reality is opened up. Of this character are the objects or qualities perceived, known as extension or space-filling, in its various forms, and what we regard as force in dynamics and other sciences.

But the meaning may be—(2.) That, in apprehending or knowing, that which is apprehended or known is always and necessarily a state of consciousness, or a form of the conscious subject itself, that nothing can ever be present to the mind but "a perception," that is, an "impression," or its copy "an idea," and consequently, that our consciousness can never transcend, so to speak, its own states, or know anything but itself. We need not here refer to the concessions made to Hume in this interpretation, as yielding him a conscious subject, or more than a conscious impression. I speak of a conscious subject and its state to make the possible interpretation really intelligible, though this is to concede him too much. Supposing this to be the meaning, and it seems to be so indisputably, whence and what is the guarantee of the remarkably broad assumption here made? It is not enough to refer to previous philosophers who may have held the view. That might suffice for a hypothetical development of its consequences. That would be taking up a tradition, and showing what it leads to. But what we have to ask is, What is the guarantee of this broad principle? Is it a generalisation from experience? Is it an *a priori* law of intelligence? No attempt is made by Hume even to answer this question. All we get is that "philosophy" and "reflection" teach us that so and so is the case. But I do not find that philosophy or reflection really teaches me anything of the sort. Besides, I must distinctly object to dealing with a psychological matter in this way. We ought not to assume at the beginning what forecloses the field of psychological inquiry—viz., as to what are the objects given or apprehended in knowledge. No sound psychology can start with an assumption as to the limitation of consciousness in the sphere of its objects. It must be open to true method to find what are the objects known as a matter of fact. And if it can be shown that there is more in consciousness, or for consciousness, than sensations or impressions more than facts, so to speak, of consciousness itself, we are bound to accept the conclusion. Any system of philosophy which professes to reproduce or reconstruct the world of knowledge and being on such an assumption, and without dealing, at the very first, with this question, is doomed to aberration and error.

It is thus quite obvious why Mr Green, among others of the school, speaks of all percepts as "feelings." In pursuance of his view that "thought" constitutes nature, it is necessary to hold all the matter or material necessary to the constitution to be within consciousness, and feeling can never be taken as the synonym of the quality of the material reality, of the qualities of things in time and space, of the unconscious and insentient. Once we have only "feelings" to deal with, to constitute into objects, we are on the high way to the making of nature by thought or consciousness working in this form. We have only to pile up the feelings, to synthesise them into an aggregate, and the thing is made. But the analysis which gives this result, if analysis there ever were, is one utterly repudiated by every sound psychology. We are back here to the sensations of Condillac and the impressions of Hume. Kant's matter, or "manifold of sense," in its dubious character is abolished, and we have the very definite subjective "feeling" installed in its room. The Hegelian extreme of spinning the particular out of thought or category is also thus avoided. The categorising spider is dispensed with, and the web of things, though somewhat thin, is woven without it.

This one premiss of Hume runs all through Neo-Kantianism. It is present in every one of the school; and it is fatal, unless vindicated, to the conclusions of all. The proof of this will be offered in the sequel.

So far as Kant is concerned, Neo-Kantians generally reject the *noumenon,* or thing-in-itself, standing by itself, and cut off from the sphere of phænomenal knowledge. They borrow Kant's relativity, but they reject his thing-in-itself. On this they may be said to be unanimous. Substantial reality of this sort is decried and denied. But the question at once arises, How is egoistic idealism in this case to be avoided? The formless unrelated sensations do not yield a standard of truth. They have even no reality, so considered. Yet it is admitted that reality does not wholly depend on the individual ego, or all individual egos put together. How am I to know whether what I relate is really so related? To fill up this gap in the system, Mr Green has recourse to an Eternal Self-consciousness, or self-distinguishing consciousness, which, while timeless, contains all the relations of the universe known and unknown to us. It is as we relate according to the relations of the eternal consciousness, that we reach the truth of things. This is an infinite fount, or, better, reservoir of timeless relations, which pours itself into the human consciousness in time. It is the condition not only of knowledge, but the creator of reality, if such a concept could be applied to an eternal act, and if any link between such an act and succession in time could be conceived. This hypothesis or metaphor we shall examine in the sequel.

Others, like M. Renouvier, while rejecting Kant's noumenon, do not adopt this view. Ignoring, as M. Renouvier does, the conscious subject in the interest of a centre of representations, and thus holding all so-called egos or subjects in time to be but centres of representations, he could not consistently hold by an eternal self-distinguishing consciousness. He boldly, therefore, substitutes for Kant's noumenon, as the true conception of being, the idea of phænomena as far as relation— in other words, the idea of relationship, or relationship in the most abstract form conceivable. What we mean by being apart from this or that relation, is simply the conception of relation in general. Relation is the category of categories, and existence in its last and highest form is relation stretched to its utmost generality. Whether such a conception can be identified with reality at all, whether, in fact, it is higher than this or that actual relation, whether it is more than a pure abstraction, dependent on the individual consciousness, whether it points to more than the mere possibility of being, are questions which we may readily put, but which the system would probably find a difficulty in answering. Being "for itself,"—that is, for relation,—is very nearly equivalent to the doctrine "being for knowledge," urged as a modification of Mr Green's view. The former expression has the advantage of greater definiteness; but all that can be urged against it applies with equal force to the latter phrase.

The main point of the controversy between Neo-Kantianism and a true Realism, is whether the reality attributed to the particulars, individuals,—in a word, the facts of experience, can be adequately expressed in the reality attributed to general ideas, whether generalisations or universal conceptions. Are the conditions under which we think a particular object precisely equivalent, in the matter of reality, to the conditions under which we perceive an object,—say of time and space, or even of our own conscious life, realised under conditions of time? The whole tendency of Neo-Kantianism is to blur the distinction under this head. It seeks to fuse, in the first place, the knowledge, called generally thought, or representation, with the object, whatever it be, thought or represented, to make, in fact, the thought an absolute, not dependent on any object separable from it, or having a proper existence of its own. It would thus draw the whole of what we understand by outward or external reality within the sphere of "thought," —that is, truly consciousness or a subjective existence. It seeks or tends, in the second place, to absorb the conscious subject or self in this same thought or general mode of conceiving things; for the conscious subject is not allowed to have any separate or independent reality apart from the thought, which is the form of its life and being, and which is a common or universal intelligence, in which it participates. The conscious subject, if, indeed, the name ought to be retained, when the thing has disappeared, is merely the conscious condition of this thought or intelligence, which is working all in all; it is the "vehicle" in which it is conveyed, or the medium through which it is revealed to the world of the finite. "The conscious subject" floats in a certain dreamland of "thought." Its reality lies in a mutual play of categories, where experience is not.

Finally, to complete the evisceration of the reality of the individual ego as even a true time existence, it turns out that it is only a form, or mode, of one Eternal Ego or self-distinguishing consciousness, which appears in every individual, that there is not "a double consciousness" in man—both an individual and an eternal ego—but simply this one self-distinguishing consciousness pervading all individualities, and making all; so that any finite reality which the Ego might be supposed to have in its actual thinking or representing is cleared away, and is replaced by a timeless reality superior to it and to all individual intelligences. And thus the circle is completed. We start with "thought;" we get rid of the independent object in the interest of thought. Thought is then promoted to the place of the conscious subject, and is credited with doing what only a thinker could do. Thought then pierces through the finite subject, and leaves him wholly behind in the interest of an eternal self-distinguishing consciousness, which is thought in its highest form. On this lofty abstraction hangs not only all knowledge, but all that we call fact in experience, the whole universe of being, all morality and all religion—in a word, "all the law and the prophets." The points at issue between this form of Idealism and Realism are mainly, (*a*) Is the abstraction implied in such a method and line of thinking, identical or convertible with the reality of experience? (*b*) Is it convertible with the extent of the facts and order of experience? (*c*) Does it afford a conception or theory adequate to the facts of our mental or conscious life? (*d*) Does it afford a conception or even hypothesis on which science can consistently mark out the order of the world, and find its laws? (*e*) Does it afford an adequate ground for a moral and religious system which still conserves the facts of morality and religion? These are the questions that now await an answer.

II.—NATURE AND CONSCIOUSNESS, AS IN MR GREEN'S 'PROLEGOMENA TO ETHICS.'

EVERY one with an adequate conception of the relations between Psychology and Metaphysics on the one hand, and Ethics proper on the other, will accept the position that the ground and possibility of a theory of moral obligation and a moral ideal for man are to be sought for in the two first-mentioned sciences. The problem of Ethics is not merely to generalise the modes of human conduct, as in actual experience; it is not simply to afford certain kinds of prudential injunctions as to action in given circumstances. The science of Ethics seeks to find the ground of moral obligation—the *rationale* of the " ought "— to exhibit the moral ideal or ideals of life, as grounded on a view of the whole nature of man.

A psychology which reduces man to a mere bodily organism, or to a series of reflex states called sensations, resulting from stimuli on this organism, may give rise to an ethics of prudence—of caution and care for the pleasure and continuance of life; it cannot ground moral obligation in any real sense of the term, and it fails as completely in exhibiting any true moral ideal. It is a worthy task, therefore, to seek in the psychology of man a ground, if that can be found, of moral obligation and moral law—facts compatible with those conceptions, and fitted to yield them a basis in reality.

But not less important than the bearing of Psychology, or an analysis of knowledge on Ethics, is its relation to the great ontological question of the being and nature of God. This question must be approached through an analysis of knowledge, and can only be determined through this analysis. Facts, data, scientific generalisations and results, are no doubt in the first place essential to the determination; but it is psychology alone, or, if the term be preferred, philosophy, meaning always an analysis of human knowledge, which can ultimately decide the question as one of reason. It is not so much facts as the interpretation of facts, through conceptions or principles, which conducts us in this sphere to the ultimate conclusion. A decision on this the highest problem of Ontology is necessary alike to the completeness of philosophy and to the satisfaction of our moral ideal. The needs alike of speculation and of human life in its practical aspect have habitually given prominence to the question, and speculative philosophy in this country and abroad has turned emphatically of late upon the reality, the nature, the conception of the supreme principle of the world—in a word, on the notion and existence of Deity.

Obviously no philosophy can pretend to the exhausting even of its own proper problems until it has faced this question, and given a deliverance on it, in one form or another. What is all reflection on experience, what all speculation, but an imperfect and broken work, unless it lead to some conception in regard to the origin and genesis of the sum of phænomena,—of the reality we know? Science may select and luxuriate in its special domains; but philosophy cannot so restrict itself, if it is to be faithful to itself. Philosophy is a view of the whole; it aspires to confront all being: and the ultimate question is not so much, *is* there a Power at the root of things—of all this phænomenal world, all this real world—as WHAT is this Power? In a word, WHAT IS GOD? How are we to think of Him? What is our worthiest and our truest conception of that Power, which our own limitation and dependence suggest to us as at least correlative with our reality, and the reality of the world?

Now I may say at once, with regard to this point, that we must from the requirements of the case have a Power, or conceive a Power, a Being, simply, if you choose, somehow in relation to us conscious beings, and to the world of nature. A Deity utterly out of relation to us, not in any way manifested to us or in us, and in the world around us, is no Deity at all,—at least, He is not one for whom we can care, as He is not one whom we can know. The true Deity must hold us in the bonds of reality, of intimate relationship. He cannot be held as standing wholly apart from us, unrevealed to us, unknown and incognisable. The main question about Deity comes to be, what precisely is the relation in which he appears to us, in which we stand to Him, in which we can know Him, and through which we can approach Him? This again means for us—What is our worthiest conception of God?

This relationship between what I would call Psychology, involving the Theory of Knowledge, and Ethics, Metaphysics, or Ontology, may be regarded as admitted by schools of quite opposite opinions and results. Nowhere is this allowed more emphatically than in the works of the late Mr T. H. Green of Oxford, with whose teaching and writings a line of speculation, somewhat novel in this country, is associated. I am quite well aware that Mr Green has objected, and very properly, to a certain kind of this analysis—that, namely, which, founding on the conceivable by us and its necessary limits—our inability to think so and so—would restrict objective reality by our limitations. And he has laid down the principle that we must look to "the determinations of being" if we are to get any sound results.[1] There is a sense in which this is an eminently legitimate method. But I fear that in his own application of the method, Mr Green has looked at "the determinations of being" mainly as conceived by us, or rather as he supposes them conceived, and that his own practice coincides pretty nearly with the vicious theory which he criticises. The same principle of method—the analysis of knowing—had, indeed, been put forward and proceeded on by Professor Ferrier of St Andrews in his *Theory of Knowing and Being*. There is a marked similarity in this respect, and generally in premisses, between the writings of these two authors, though there may be perceived a certain difference in result. Mr Green, however, shows a closer connection with certain positions of Kant and the general drift of Hegel than

[1] See *Works*, vol. iii. p. 143.

Professor Ferrier, at least, in the *Theory of Knowing and Being;* and what is foreign in Ferrier appears in a more national dress than in Green, as it certainly stands out in an incomparably clearer style.

Abroad there has been a tendency in the same line of thinking. Without referring to all who might be named, it is sufficient to point to the writings of M. Renouvier, under the headings of Logic and Psychology. He is perhaps the ablest and the most thoroughgoing of all the authors who may be classed under the title of Neo-Kantians. And it is but just to say that, besides his remarkable ability, he is open to recognition of those broad facts of experience, which are so severe a test of the real application of the doctrines of the school. He certainly has too large a share of the French logical habit and its general soundness of reflection, to suppose that facts, otherwise doomed to disappearance on the principles of the system, could be saved by the metaphor of an Eternal Consciousness.

Mr Green, in his Introduction to the *Prolegomena to Ethics,* accepts emphatically the position of an analysis of knowledge as necessary to Ethics. And the aim of his investigations may be said to be to vindicate the grounds at once of obligation and the moral ideal. And it cannot be alleged that he does not dig deep enough, for he goes back to questions as to the very nature of man, consciousness, and reality; he offers a theory on those points, and he is of opinion that this theory affords the ground of freedom, moral obligation, moral law, and the highest moral ideal. Whether his psychological and metaphysical views actually afford such a ground, whether even they are consistent with the conceptions they are said to sustain, are of course questions to be considered. The main purpose, however, of these essays is not so much the consideration of those questions, as a statement and examination of the views themselves regarded as to their own grounds or guarantee and their internal consistency. If they are deficient in these respects, the question as to their compatibility with the moral ideas will be superseded. It may possibly be found that while a purely sensational psychology is too low a ground for personality or individuality, which is at the root of all ethical conception, an absolute idealism may on the other side be equally inadequate, as ultimately sweeping away the personality which it professes to establish. It may prove merely

> "Vaulting ambition which o'erleaps itself,
> And falls on the other side."

But my present purpose is not to pursue the examination of the logical results of Mr Green's theory of knowledge as bearing on Ethics. I propose merely to examine, in the first instance, his theory or 'Metaphysics of Knowing,' and that mainly as it is presented in the three introductory chapters of the *Prolegomena to Ethics*, and the bearing of this theory on the highest problem of ontology — our conception of the nature and reality of Deity. We have in these chapters a definite theory of Knowing, and its application to ontology in its highest department, — a theory which certainly has results of the greatest concern and the widest reach. The exposition is the most consecutive, and, I think, the clearest, which Mr Green has left us of his views on this subject. And it is desirable in the interests of speculative truth to subject them to examination and discussion.

There are three main points in Mr Green's treatment of the 'Metaphysics of Knowing.' There is, first of all, the question of the relation of Man to Nature, and what is implied in a knowledge of nature. With this is connected the analysis of knowledge in what we call Perception.

There is, secondly, an analysis of the meaning and application of Reality as conceived by us.

There is, thirdly, his doctrine of knowledge as Relational.

These points are not treated by him quite separately, but they are the lines along which his speculation travels with a view to determine the nature of the finite self-consciousness, and, as a final conclusion, the nature of the eternal or infinite self-consciousness with which he connects the ultimate reality of man and things. It will be my endeavour to state his views, following, as far as possible, the order of their development, and to examine their truth and value.

The first question with Mr Green in his analysis of knowledge may be said to be the relation of man to nature, and what is implied in a knowledge of nature. In stating his opinion on this and other points, I shall adhere as closely as I can to his own language,—ordinary terms being frequently so used by him as to require careful scrutiny of the meaning. There is not unfrequently a double sense of a term which is even self-inconsistent.

Mr Green starts with the question: "Can the knowledge of nature be itself a part or product of nature?" (p. 13). From the terms of this question it might seem that it is assumed that "knowledge" and "nature" are two separate things, that there is a reference to the qualities of what we call the world of the senses, that the question is whether "nature." as a sense-object is the source of our knowledge as a product. But this is not quite what is meant. The question is qualified by the phrase, "in that sense of nature in which it is said to be an object of knowledge" (p. 11). And we are told that if the question be answered in the negative, then "man in respect of the function called knowledge is not merely a child of nature" (p. 11). And there is in him "a principle not natural, and a specific function of this principle is rendering knowledge possible" (p. 11).

It may be supposed that knowledge or consciousness arises from what we call "matter and motion," but we are here told that these have no existence *per se*,—these being objects of consciousness. They do not exist "otherwise than as related to a consciousness." And it seems to be maintained that "matter" means only "a statement of relations between facts in the way of feeling, or between objects that we present to ourselves as sources of feeling" (p. 12). "Motion," too, means "a synthesis of the different positions successively held by one and the same body," and "position" or "succession" of a body and its "identity" mean "relations of what is contained in experience, through which alone that content possesses a definite character and becomes a connected whole" (p. 14).

Matter and motion, therefore, as known or in a consciousness, are relations apparently of something called feeling or feelings. They do not exist *per se*—at least, they have no meaning for us when we so speak of them. That which exists for consciousness, that which we know, is a relation or series of relations. But a relation needs "a principle of union." What, then, is that principle which renders a relation possible? This cannot be a relation itself, for a relation results from a principle of union. It must be the source of a connected experience "which renders both the nature that we know and our knowledge of it possible." "In a man who can know a nature there is a principle which is not natural, and which cannot be explained as we explain the facts of nature" (p. 14).

This definition of matter given by Mr Green is as inadequate and assumptive a statement as could well be made. It seems that matter — that is, perceived or known matter — consists in "relations between facts in the way of feeling, or between objects that we present to ourselves as sources of feeling" (p. 13). We might very fairly here ask the question, What are the things called "facts" between which, "the relations" subsist? They are apparently "facts" "in the way of feeling." Surely any tyro in psychology would know that this is not an indisputable point — that to identify "the facts" of sense with the "feelings" of sense is exactly what psychology has not been doing for a hundred years at least, and that the main burden of the question of perception lies in the distinction contended for between things called qualities or percepts of what is a not-self, and the feelings and sensations of the conscious subject. All this is slurred over in a single phrase, and matter is defined "as relations between facts in the way of feeling." Surely it is worth considering that a point of limit between the sentient and the insentient in sense-experience is a main contention of Realism.

But let us seek to realise for a moment what is included under the term "feeling," as employed by Mr Green. It obviously takes in all that we find, apprehend, or know directly in Sense-Perception,—all, as we say, that is presented to us in sense. It embraces tastes, odours, muscular feelings, feeling of contact, sounds, colours, &c. Along with these it indicates equally, extension, solidity, figure,—all the qualities we perceive and conceive as essential to material reality. The term, as thus applied, slurs over the most important distinctions in connection with the objects of Sense-Perception. One would imagine, from Mr Green's use of it, that he was wholly unaware of psychological discussion and inquiry on this point from the time of Locke and Hume to our own day.

Owing in great measure to certain assumptions, really *prejudicia*, judgments formed beforehand as to the immediate object of sense-perception, we have had a series of philosophical theories regarding this object, from Descartes downwards. All proceed on an assumption, not proved, not warranted by the facts of the case, viz., that what we directly or immediately apprehend in sense is always and only a state of the conscious percipient, or, at the utmost, some ideal, or in modern language, psychical phænomenon. Sense-knowledge has been held to be a relation between similars. If we suppose the two factors, perceiver and percept, to be of different natures, it is held that there can be no perception or knowledge. This was an assumption unworthy alike of science and philosophy—of the principles of every sound investigation into fact or truth. Yet it has been most prevailing, and it subsists now, exercising as baneful an influence as ever it did. It is a case in which a so-called "theory of knowledge" is made to usurp the prerogatives of actual psychological observation and analysis; it is to set up certain pretentious "conditions" of knowledge as dominating knowledge itself.

With Descartes it issued in his doctrine of mental "ideas"—modes simply of the mind of the percipient, which he was supposed to perceive, in lieu of an actually existing extended object. This "idea," however, represented it; and God being veracious, the actual extended world did, or at least, as he says, might, exist as pictured in the idea. Besides the idea representative of the primary qualities, there was sensation; this, too, being simply a state of the consciousness.

Then we have precisely the same assumption in Locke. We perceive things not immediately, but only by the intervention of the ideas we have of them. Ideas of the qualities of bodies, that is, the primary qualities, are images, real resemblances of what are in bodies — extension, solidity, figure, mobility, &c. Sensations, as of colour, sound, taste, smell, have no resemblance to their outward causes—certain powers of bodies. They are simply states of consciousness. Ideas and sensations are, however, equally ideal or psychical facts. Locke's use of "idea" is no doubt thoroughly ambiguous. It means any object of thought whatever, including (1) the object in perception; (2) the object in imagination; (3) the abstraction we make from things, irrespective altogether of their existence. But it is always an ideal phænomenon.

Then, with Berkeley we have the keeping up of Locke's ideas, but the denial of their representative character. There is, according to Berkeley, no world or set of material things or qualities beyond the ideas. Not only do ideas not correspond to such an entity as a material world; it does not exist in addition to the idea. Minds, and ideas in minds, are all that is. All the objects we perceive have their continued existence or subsistence only in mind. The idea with Berkeley is obviously a psychical fact or phænomenon, though he is generally regarded as holding it different from a state of consciousness. It is *in* the mind, not *of* the mind. And he tells us that "ideas" are "real things." "Ideas imprinted on the senses by the Author of Nature are called real things; and those excited in the imagination, being less regular, vivid, and constant, are more properly termed *ideas* or *images* of things, which they copy and represent. But then our sensations, be they never so vivid and distinct, are nevertheless ideas; that is, they exist in the mind, or are perceived by it, as truly as the ideas of its own framing."¹

There is thus no difference in kind between "ideas" of sense and those of imagination or memory,—none between ideas and sensations. All are equally psychical or ideal facts, call them what you will, differing only in degree or vivacity. Of course, the inference from this, that the *percipi* of an idea is its *esse*, is obvious, that it cannot resemble anything but an idea, that it exists only in a mind, and can subsist only in a mind, supposing it to have a continuous existence at all. No percept, be it extension, solidity, heat, or cold, can be separated from perception in some mind. They are, as psychical facts, on an equal level. The substantial reality of the physical world was thus gone, and not less, as seems to me, its material phænomenal reality. Second causes, too, in perception had disappeared; God was put in the place of nature: to Him is directly attributable all our sense-impressions,—sensations and ideas,—and creation with Berkeley came to mean, as has been said, "that God decreed from that time to produce ideas in the minds of finite spirits, in that order and according to those rules which we call the laws of Nature."² It should be

---

[1] *Principles of Human Knowledge*, sec. 33.
[2] Reid, *Works*, p. 287.

noticed here that Berkeley did not deny the non-perceived reality of the idea, simply because it was an object of perception, and, therefore, involved a relation of knowledge, but because of its nature as an ideal or psychical fact, capable thus only of existing in a mind or consciousness.

Hume's impression came readily out of Berkeleyanism. This is psychical, wholly psychical: a conscious state only, however, not a state of consciousness, for that would imply a continuous consciousness, and thus a permanent conscious subject. The substantial reality of the material world had gone with Berkeley; the substantial reality of the other factor in knowledge—mind or finite mind—was also now to go with Hume. And existence is to be translated by an impression, at the best by a series of impressions or consciousnesses, illegitimately bound together in a series. This is the stage at which Mr Green takes up the point; and he proposes to restore knowledge and reality by binding together in relations, necessary relations, the "impressions," the "feelings," to each other in an unalterable objective sequence, and to a self-distinguishing consciousness, as the subjective ground of the objective relations. This, at least, in the first place. But he has not one word of question for the position that the immediate object of sense-perception is necessarily psychical, far less for the assumption on which the whole modern theories on this point have been grounded, and unwarrantably grounded. And it may be confidently added that Kant's "phænomena" are in no better plight than Hume's "impressions" or Green's "feelings."

Now all this has been questioned—this assumption, and its effect in the consequent limitation of perception to psychical or ideal facts. "I perceive the external object," says Reid, "and I perceive it to exist." There are "things in the mind and things *external* to the mind. . . . Everything is said to be in the mind of which the mind is the subject. . . . Excepting the mind itself, and things in the mind, all other things are said to be external. . . . This distinction is not meant to signify the place of the things we speak of, but their subject."[1] In other words, I apprehend or am conscious of that which is not a state of my consciousness,—which is not a "feeling," of which I am the subject or which inheres in me, but which is the quality of a not-self or non-ego, now and here existing,—in contrast or antithesis to me, the percipient. There is no medium or mediate object; and the object perceived is not a psychical phæno-

[1] Reid, *Works*, p. 221.

menon. So much even said Berkeley, but he meant by object the idea, as actually existing,—a psychical fact,—a mental fact, however described. And Hamilton, in his later view, makes an advance on Reid. He, too, held the immediate object in perception not to be psychical; but he did not hold it to be a quality of a material world existing beyond the bodily organism, unless in the case of a resisting force. He regarded it as a quality of the organism itself, endowed with sentiency, and existing as extended. Yet the perceived object while conditioned by the sentiency of the organism, is not a "feeling," "impression," or psychical fact at all—not a state of consciousness, not an ideal phænomenon revealed to mind, but a physical quality of a physical object, the extension of the environing bodily organism. And probably in this will be found to a great extent the conciliation of the two opinions—the view that what we perceive is psychical alone, with the view that what we perceive is truly physical or material,—the physical being thus brought, as it were, into immediate relationship to that mind which certainly permeates the bodily organism with its power of sentiency. The object perceived with Hamilton is internal; still it is not mental, but physical or material. But all this development and progress of analytical psychology is wholly ignored by Mr Green. He seems completely ignorant of it, and speaks and writes as if psychological history had been arrested at Hume's impression, which he baptises "feeling." And the same may be said of all of his school to the present time.

What further, it may be asked, would a scientific man in these times say to a writer who thinks that the term *feeling* appropriately and fully describes material forces and their effects,—mechanical, chemical, electrical, biological? The transmutations of energy, the evolutions of the forces at work in the sensible world or sphere of science, organism, and life, are to be regarded as feelings, or, at the utmost, as feelings and their relations. Would the scientific man not at once say this is an inappropriate and utterly misleading piece of nomenclature?

But there is much more than this to be said from the scientific point of view. The one great achievement of recent science has been the connecting of our sensations and perceptions, the former as mental states and the objects of the latter, with forms of matter which wholly transcend both sensation and perception. Psychology had long ago pointed out the dependence of sensation, especially sound and colour, on things unfelt and unperceived, on, in a word, the supersensible in the act of vision and hearing. The vibratory motion which precedes or accompanies sound, the undulatory motion which precedes or accompanies vision, and is totally unfelt, unperceived, and unknown to the conscious subject who experiences the vision or hearing, — all this was the commonplace of psychology. And this alone was sufficient to show that the insensible, the imperceptible, as a reality, accompanied, was implied in sense-action—that it *was*, while wholly unknown to us. But modern science has revealed to us the great space-filling thing called ether, and beyond this the atomic realities at the root of all material reality. It has revealed, too, the transformation of force in the form of motion into sense-objects as perceived by us. All this it has done. It has, in fact, discovered to us "those secret powers" which may be attributed to the primary qualities of body as causing sensation. All this action is, however, wholly unfelt by us, unperceived by us, beyond immediate knowledge; yet it *is* during the immediate knowing. How, then, can it be said that there are not objects of knowledge which are not psychical, or simply states of consciousness? No finite consciousness whatever ever perceives these. In no finite consciousness whatever are they states; yet they have reality, and the states of consciousness would not have reality without them. They are the dominating reality in our sensations and perceptions; they are before our sensations; they are at least their partial causes. What, then, becomes of an attempt to include the whole world of actual and possible objects of sense, nay, of objects in general, in "feelings," "psychical states," states of consciousness? And if we did not know more than a mere state of consciousness in perception, how should we ever be led to refer anything in the end to ether, the space-filling,—to what is entirely out of ourselves? Why, if we know nothing but the mental, should we ever go beyond the mental, ourselves, our mind, or consciousness? How could we suppose or infer from a simple state of consciousness or sensation anything not in the least felt or perceived, wholly non-sensational, as ether in space, or molecules far back in time? How could we even, on such a supposition, have the idea of the non-sensational at all?

But the implied connotation of the term "feeling" is as misleading as the ambiguity of its application. Feeling certainly has a subjective reference and suggestion. Sensations, emotions, are especially the states or forms of a consciousness,—the experience of a sentient and conscious subject. We do not regard these as the properties of a material reality. We do not regard the insentient and unconscious as capable of or having feeling. But as the question really is as to whether there is an ultimate distinction between sentient and insentient, conscious and unconscious, as matter of fact or reality, a writer has no right to make use of a word which actually implies the identity of property in those opposites. In doing so he is guilty simply of an illogical assumption.

The bearing of this assumption on the argument is seen the moment we come to distinguish time and space and their contents. Feeling may probably be applied to what has reality and degree in time, to simple succession apart from coexistence; but if we add coexistence and mutual externality of points in space, feeling does not properly apply. No doubt there may be coexisting feelings, but it is not therefore to be assumed that coexisting points in space are simply coexisting feelings in consciousness, much less feelings in succession.

If these fundamental points, as alleged by Mr Green, be self-evident, as they are assumed to be, for practically no proof is given of them, the marvel is why such a question as to whether knowledge is a part of nature, or even a product of nature, can be put at all. If what we call nature in all its forms be simply conscious relations, while there is not even a recognition of the separate reality of the terms of the relations, what is the meaning or relevancy of asking such a question as whether knowledge is a product of nature? Such a question implies that nature is something by itself, and can produce some other thing called knowledge. But if nature be simply relations, conscious relations, nature is already knowledge, and probably as it is relations in consciousness, apart from terms, a very irrational sort of knowledge. If "matter and motion," the ultimate things in nature, be conscious relations,— relations existing only as known to consciousness, what is the use of asking the question as to whether knowledge or consciousness can be a product of these? They are already consciousness and knowledge, and the question is absurd. It means simply, Can consciousness be a part or product of itself? If motion be not a thing in itself, actual reality existing as motion, if it be only a sensation of sight and touch, dependent on our or a consciousness, then, of course, there can be no question whatever as to whether motion is the cause of thought or consciousness. Thought or consciousness is, ere or as motion is, for this is merely a form of perception, having existence only as perceived; and to say that it is the cause of perception or thought, is simply to say that perception or thought is the cause of itself Clearly, if motion is only a form of thought, or mode of thought, it never can be the cause of that which makes it. The burden of proof is shifted to the point as to whether motion can absolutely be described as a form of perception, or wholly dependent for its reality on perception.

It would be curious to know whence Mr Green supposes we get this nature or series of changes *minus* consciousness of which he speaks, and, at least, supposes as an object of our thought. If a series of changes *minus* consciousness has neither meaning nor reality, how do we get the notion of it? We can quite understand what it means. There is no use saying the words have no meaning. It is certainly an object of conception at least. And Mr Green, when he reasons about it, must admit so much. But if it never was found as separate from the understanding, and if the understanding was never found as separate from it, it is rather puzzling to discover whence we reached the concept of it. And on the very same principle, it is a puzzle to know how we got the conception of an understanding which cannot be conceived or exist apart from this related nature, and which yet makes it.

"Matter" means only "a statement of relations between facts in the way of feeling, or between objects that we present to ourselves as sources of feeling." What, we may ask, is really meant here? Is it meant that we know facts, or, in Mr Green's language, present feelings to ourselves as facts, and then relate them to each other? Are the facts then terms, known terms of the relations? Or are they only as they are in the relations? Or are they themselves relations? By-and-by we may come to have some light on those points. It may be found that relations are simply postulated that facts or terms may be at all in knowledge. We may find that the whole doctrine of relationship is reversed, in order to make the relation found the facts, and not the facts, as terms, the relation.

But clearly, if we are to take the statement in its obvious and natural meaning, we should have more in the world, objectively regarded, than relations; we should have the facts or the feelings as terms of the relations. And this admission or result would land us in a wholly different kind of philosophical view from that towards which Mr Green is laboriously working. To put as an alternative the relation of objects to consciousness, does not in the least help us here. This is a wholly different point; and what we are concerned to know is whether Mr Green regards every object known in the external world as a relation, or whether he admits there are facts and relations.

One is certainly surprised that, on a point so vital to his whole system as this doctrine of relation, he should have been at so small pains to make his doctrine explicit, or to give reasons for it. What he has not done has, however, been attempted by another whose general cast of thinking is not unlike his own. It is said that "matter" is relative, or cannot be analysed so as not to involve a relation. "Every true datum," we are told by M. Renouvier, "is synthetic — that is, capable of analysis. But analysis separates elements of a composite comparatively, not simply simple, because none of the elements can be objectified without condition and apart from every other. So that in each part we can always find a whole."[1]

Further, it is contended that all external objects are composite, because they all participate of space, time, and motion. Consciousness is not simple, for it is its function to relate to a simple

[1] Renouvier, *Essai de Critique générale ; Traité de Logique générale.* Second edition, p. 79.

representation, in all moments, an indefinite number of other agglomerated representations of every nature. Simple sensations are compound; colour is extended; sound endures in time. We cannot represent colour without surface. Analysis distinguishes, but does not make the synthesis less inevitable.[1]

This argument, applied to material reality, amounts to saying that because sensations—viz., colour, odour, taste, muscular pressure, &c.—cannot be perceived or conceived by us out of relation to space or time, each sensation is necessarily composite as a relation. The answer is obvious and simple. Each sensation is not necessarily composite; it is not necessarily a whole capable of further analysis. If we did analyse it, it would cease to be a sensation, or the sensation it is. It is impossible for us to analyse the sensation of colour into anything but itself, and yet retain the conception of colour; and so with odour, taste, resistance, muscular pressure. These are not wholes in any proper sense of the word. They are the terms, the ultimate terms, of our experience, on one of its sides, and so unanalysable and irreducible. Even when science comes to show us that sensation is partly de-

---

[1] Renouvier, *Essai de Critique générale; Traité de Logique générale*. Second edition, p. 106.

pendent on antecedent movement, undulating, vibrating, or other, it does not show us that this is involved in the conception of sensation. Sensation is not a composite in respect of this. It is there as a wholly distinct conception which we know and feel, whether we know antecedent conditions or not; and out of these we should never be able to evolve it, as back to them we should never be able to reduce it. Even the test of one conception being actually involved in another is in no way fulfilled.

Further, it may be perfectly true that in our actual perception, or even conception, we are not able to separate colour from extension, or sound from time. That does not prove that the conception of colour is composite or reducible, or that sound is in the same position. These two concepts or percepts may stand to each other in indissoluble relation; that does not make each a relation, it only makes them terms of a relation—a wholly different fact. They are still as conceptions wholly simple—" simply simple "—dependent, as such, on nothing anterior, and capable of being explained by nothing anterior. The synthesis may be inseparable, but it is a synthesis of elements which cannot be identified with each other, which are alongside each other but not the same. In the synthesis you may by abstraction separate the elements, but the elements you cannot by any abstraction or analysis separate, because they are no longer divisible wholes, but indivisible units. Every simple sensation is such; and extension and time are, while composed, the one of points out of points, the other of points in succession, utterly meaningless beyond this expression of content. It would certainly be a very pretty doctrine to maintain that because certain things are not conceivable apart by us, the things themselves are wholes. In other words, because they make up wholes, they are themselves wholes. As to colour and extension, for example, or sound and time, not being conceivable apart by us, there is an obvious confusion of the general and the particular; there is the raising of the actual relation to the rank of a general or universal necessary relation, and so applying it to particular cases in which it does not at all hold. It is quite conceivable that the same surface should be in succession red, yellow, and green, though we cannot conceive it apart from some clothing of colour. There is no necessary relation between *this* or *that* colour and *this* surface. There is a necessary relation between *some* colour and *this* surface.[1] But if each given colour and surface can be conceived without the other, what becomes of

---

[1] On this point see Ott, *L'Idéalisme*, I. c. 1, § 3.

the argument that in perception, the actual colour and the actual surface we perceive are necessarily composite and related? Is this not to carry out to absurdity the mischievous doctrine of the identity of function between perception and conception?

Of course, it may be said that although the terms of the whole of relation, in the case of colour and extension, are not themselves wholes, they are yet parts of a whole—viz., coloured-extension. But, in the first place, this is to give up the position that the natural object is ultimately a relation, and for relation to substitute term of a relation—viz., part of whole; and in the second place, if we regard the part as having its whole reality in being the part, we unwarrantably identify a particular relationship in which it happens to stand with the whole reality of the term related; and, in the third place, we commit the fallacy of what may be called the see-saw contradiction; we make the part real only as or after we relate it, while we need the part to be, and to be real, ere we can take a step in relating it.

Mr Green apparently identifies the phrase "related to consciousness" with "knowledge of phænonema," "correlation of object and subject"; and from the assertion that " relation to a subject is necessary to make an object," infers "that an object which no consciousness presented to itself would not be an object at all." In other words, he takes one side of the doctrine of phænomenal knowledge, the side which declares the necessity of an object in knowledge, and infers, in the way of the *ad dictum simpliciter* fallacy, that unless an object be in a consciousness or for a consciousness, unless it be a known object, it is not an object at all, as no object unknown to a consciousness exists. But there is a twofold fallacy here. In the first place, the known object, or object for the subject in the theory of phænomenal knowledge, is not the presented object merely, or the perceived object or quality, but all that such a perceived object suggests, or can be shown to imply in regard to reality beyond itself objectively, on which it is or may be dependent for its presentation to us. The whole object in phænomenal knowledge is not, therefore, the known object in the sense of the perceived or apprehended object in a given time, but what to thought surrounds and conditions it. And it cannot be inferred from saying that the perceived object is necessary to knowledge, that the ground of the perception is "not an object at all." In fact, this would not be a reasoning, but a simple tautology. The perceived (or conscious) object must be a perceived (or conscious) object; hence an object unperceived (or beyond consciousness) is not an object at all. So far as my consciousness is concerned, I thus know that the definitely known object, or, if you choose, experienced object, is not the whole object; in fact, suggests an object, or portion of existence, unperceived, but still existing.

In the second place, even if it were true that I can put no meaning into "an object," unless as it actually stands in relation to a consciousness, unless as actually known, this would but imply that I transfer, and must transfer, the meaning of a term in my knowledge to all the knowledge I can conceive. It does not imply that this meaning belongs to all things which exist, as they exist. It does not even imply that my knowledge is the measure of all knowledge, that my form of knowledge is the form of the knowledge of every intelligent being. There is here the assumption of absolute knowledge on my part,— the identifying of me and my knowing with the essence of all knowing. A philosophy which starts with such an assumption has completed its work; but as it has done it by an assumption, it has done nothing. There is, in a word, in all this an illegitimate passage from psychology to ontology.

In the third place, is it meant to be contended that no object exists which is not in actual relation to a consciousness? If so, objects spring into being only with each successive conscious act, and they not less drop out of being with each successive conscious act. Consciousness, therefore, either creates objects as it goes along, to drop each out of being for a successor; or objects somehow spring up just of themselves into consciousness or being, through some curious pre-established harmony between the march of events and the steps of consciousness. The author's theory or hypothesis, that there is "an eternal consciousness," that is, a consciousness not in time, for which all objects exist, and which are thus held in being, need not be considered at this point. It could easily be shown that such a hypothesis, or personified abstraction, never can by any possibility touch the conscious order or succession of events in time; and it matters nothing to the argument whether there be one or many time-subjected consciousnesses in the world. If actual existence of an object be only as it is in relation to a consciousness, this existence is either a creation of the consciousness, or a pre-established harmony of an independent order of things.

In the fourth place, is it allowed that there

may be knowable objects not yet in actual relation to a consciousness? Is that held to be an object, which is capable merely of being related to a consciousness, yet not at this moment known to any consciousness? What, then, becomes of the position that there is no object at all which is not related to a consciousness? Or that actual relation to a consciousness is convertible with object?

All possible objects are not, it is admitted, actually in or for this or that individual consciousness; they are not in and for the consciousness of all the individuals on this planet at this moment. No single individual consciousness, no totality of individual consciousnesses, contains at this moment all the knowable, even in time. New objects, new relations, are lying undoubtedly undiscovered; others discovered are unthought of or forgotten. Have these no reality? Are they not in existence? At length they come, for the first time, into 'the consciousness of this or that individual. Do they now, for the first time, come into being? And when they are recovered after oblivion, are they revealed? The admission that there are knowable objects, new and undiscovered,—the veriest knowable relation of the meanest insect in the sunlight,—destroys the whole essence of a theory which makes existence for a consciousness, that is, known existence, convertible with all existence. To try to meet this point, as has been done, by saying that all objects, that is, relations, exist in one Eternal Consciousness, above time, in which there is no succession, is of no use. If this statement were intelligible, which it is not, it would not affect the reality of knowable objects in a consciousness subject to succession, or enable us to understand how an object can both be described as existing only as a known object, and yet existing as a merely knowable, that is, as yet unknown, object.

But what really is the foundation of all this talk? On what ground is it alleged that there is nothing "outside of consciousness"; that there are objects in consciousness outside of each other, but none, no being, outside of consciousness itself? The statement is generally advanced as a principle, in fact, a mere assumption. But when we analyse its ground, we find that it depends wholly on a definition, and a limited definition, of object. This is restricted to object of actual knowledge, or known object. An object is regarded as the correlative of subject, and of conscious subject; and so, given an object, there must be a subject or knower. Of course, with this as a definition, the conclusion is foreclosed,—that an object is only for knowledge or consciousness; that it is not outside consciousness as known. But this is either a simple begging of the real point at issue, or a trifling with the whole matter. It is true that a known object is in or for consciousness or knowledge, though even here the question is always open, What is the nature of each object known, and what are the kinds of objects? Are these modes of matter or mind, or is there only one kind of object known to consciousness? But, admitting that a known object is always an object for consciousness, it does not follow that a known object is all that exists, or that that which may become an object of knowledge at a future time has absolutely no reality. It has as yet no known reality; but we are not entitled on this ground to assert that reality there is not, because reality known to us is always necessarily an object for consciousness. This would be to assume the very point at issue, that there is no reality in nature or fact apart from known reality. Nay, it is true that known reality falls out of the known or knowing, as in the case of memory. A past object that has been known by us is, or may be, existent now, though it has fallen out of our perception, even knowledge. We should be guilty of unwarrantable dogmatism in saying either that the object does not now exist because it is no longer known to us as an actual reality of space and time, or that if it exists at all, it must exist as known by some subject, individual, finite or infinite. This is wholly to go beyond any premiss we have laid down, and simply to assume that a certain definition of object, or of object in a certain relation, extends to all actual and possible objects of knowledge. What is true of the past holds of the future, and all the possibilities of knowing. These never can be limited by the conditions of actual knowledge, and reality, therefore, cannot be circumscribed by a narrow and arbitrary definition.

We know certain facts connected with our sense-experience with perfect certainty. We know (1) that there is a nerve-current preceding actual or conscious sensation and perception by us, of which at the moment we are wholly unconscious. We come to infer it from scientific investigation, from observation, and inductive inference. We know (2), also, that beyond the organism or bodily sphere there are agencies in space which precede, condition, so far determine our actual sensation or perception, of which, however, we have neither sensation nor perception. There is the vibration of the air in sound; there is the undulation of ether in vision. These are objects neither of sensation nor perception; they are never apprehended by us as such; they are simply suggestions, inferences, needed to account for the actual facts of sense of which we are conscious. They accompany the actual conscious state, but they lie wholly beyond it; they transcend it: they are not perceptible by us, and never will be perceptible by us so long as our senses are limited as they now are. What then? What follows directly from this?

Surely it will not be maintained that categorising this insensible object after it has actually performed its function in sensation on our consciousness, and may have quite ceased to be in the form it was—conceiving it now, when it is inferred, as in time and space and as cause—made it an object of our consciousness at the time of its occurrence or action, now past and gone? Does my thinking or conceiving this insensible, imperceptible thing, called vibration or undulation, make it to have been simply a mode of or in my consciousness, when I know as a matter of fact it was not and never could be any such thing? Clearly this thing can exist apart from our consciousness, during the moment of actual perception of its sensible effect: we come to know this afterwards, that it *did* exist during our perception or sensation, though we knew nothing of it at the time. If, therefore, its existence depends on its being intuited in time and space, and categorised, this existence must be intuited and categorised by another consciousness than ours. This existence is now a past existence; and if it needed intuition and category to hold it in being, it was held in being by some consciousness of mind not ours. On what possible ground can we assert that this was so? Is there any need that this insensible thing called ether or undulatory motion, which, unconsciously to us, acted on our organism, and so far produced sensation, was, while it acted, the object of a consciousness not ours? Why should this consciousness let it out of itself to act on ours? Why did it not keep it to itself? This may be because, when I afterwards come to infer its existence from sensible data, I think it as having been in time and space, and as cause. But have I any ground whatever, from the fact that I am led to infer insensible ether as the cause of sensation, to suppose that it must have existed in a consciousness at all? I now know that it did exist in space and time at the moment I experienced the sensation, but I did not know this at the time. What is there more to lead me to suppose that it existed in a consciousness, and one necessarily like my own, which perceived it in time and space, and as cause of my sensation?—like mine, no doubt, as to categorising, but endowed with a power of perception indefinitely greater than mine, capable of perceiving what utterly transcends my power of perception? What is this but a cumbrous, useless, incompetent hypothesis? Why should I duplicate my consciousness? And how, if I do, should this numerically different consciousness perceive it as the cause of my sensation? The, to me, imperceptible undulation might be an object of perception to it, but what should it know of my perception? The assertion that there is nothing outside of consciousness is thus belied by the simplest sense-experience.

Mr Green's conclusion is, that in order to know an object — that is, a relation, there is needed the existence or action of something not in nature, not in the order of relations, not itself a relation, not an object in time. This, we may say broadly, is consciousness, as it is in the individual, and ultimately a supreme or one Eternal Consciousness. This consciousness in man and in the universe is the same, only working under different conditions. But we have first to deal with it as in man; for it will surely be admitted, even by Mr Green, that to know this one Eternal Consciousness, we must know it first in its human aspect, or as subjected to the limitations of the animal organism, with which, as we shall see, the Eternal Consciousness has a fruitless and baffled struggle.

With this is connected the further position that consciousness, in knowing the object-relation, makes it. A self-distinguishing consciousness knows something, an object, a relation, and in so knowing makes it; for it has existence only as related to consciousness, or as consciousness relates it.

"The consciousness through which alone nature exists for us is neither natural nor a result of nature." "What is the "nature" here spoken of, whether simply assumed or allowed to be? Evidently it is given as opposed to consciousness, that is, the consciousness of it by us. As yet we know no other consciousness. This nature will mean, then, a process simply of change, or a series of events, minus consciousness. It is also used as identical with "experience." If this nature be known by us to be, the consciousness by which we know the process of change cannot be one stage or any event in the changing process; it must be that which remains all through the change, conscious of each point, and conscious thus of the whole. In plain language, change in time, to be known, requires a knower, one and identical through the change. The use of the abstract term "consciousness" for this is, I must note in passing, an inappropriate expression. This "consciousness," however, is described as neither natural nor a result of nature. It is not natural simply in the narrow sense of nature, or the conception of nature, as already defined. But it is, as thus used, a misleading expression. The nature spoken of has, it is maintained, no existence for us unless as in this consciousness; and yet it is contrasted with consciousness as being natural, while consciousness is at the same time spoken of as something not natural,—over and above nature. If nature does not exist for us until we are conscious of it, and only as we are conscious of it, consciousness, the one side of the complexus, is just as natural as nature, the other side, is, or nature is just as non-natural as consciousness is. The contrast between nature and consciousness as two things, even conceptions, has ceased to have a meaning.

The fatal flaw in all this reasoning is this: The thing, the object, has no existence in itself; therefore it cannot generate the subject called thought. But, on the other hand, the subject, the thought, has no existence in itself; therefore it cannot generate the object or thing, indeed generate anything. How, then, can aught be known? How can there be a relation of knowledge at all? If there be no object to begin with, and no subject to begin with, who is to start the business of knowing? "The understanding creates nature;" but nature equally creates the understanding, for neither is until the other is. If they come together so that there is knowledge, which is creation, some one must surely help them. Knowledge is a relation; and as each term is helpless to constitute it, and only really exists as related, there is some higher cause or power which brings them together, or rather which evolves the relation in which they both exist, and only exist. But the producer of a relation which creates at once the relation and the terms, primarily the first, secondarily the latter, is something of which we, as being merely in relation, can form no conception.

But this "nature" created by the understanding has in itself, as a nature, no distinct or continued existence. It is dependent on the understanding, —in a word, on mind or self, at first the individual self, working on certain material. But I do not find that this understanding or individual ego has any distinct or continuous being apart from that nature which stands related to it, or which it relates to itself, and so constitutes.

It is spoken of as the understanding, and also a self-distinguishing consciousness; but I do not find any provision made for the beginning of its distinguishing or constituting act. I do not find any provision made for the self as simply a potency, which comes into act. On the contrary, when it is first known, or is known as existent, it is already linked to nature, inseparately related to it. Apart from this relation, it is a meaningless abstraction, or rather meaningless term. How, then, am I to say that it constitutes nature, or does anything whatever in the way of cognitive activity? If the object of its act does not exist until it makes it, or rather, until it and the object coexist, how am I entitled to say that the self-distinguishing ego is the superior of the two, or that it makes nature? Does not nature equally make it, if there is any making in the case? The whole doctrine is a see-saw of mutually destructive contradictories. If you give the complex understanding + nature a consciousness, it will be a consciousness of a complex distinguished as to its terms, so made, but made already, not to make by a self-distinguishing consciousness. We have now got into the high blaze of fusion, —the strong heat under which the factors of the problem are dissolved. Understanding disappears in nature; nature in understanding. There is a new compound, which is both or neither, as you choose to take it.

But there are questions regarding the function of "nature" in knowledge which it would have been well had Mr Green, when he raised this question, thought proper to discuss. It is true that we find in knowledge subject and object, or subject and nature. Is this properly described as simply the relation of a self-distinguishing consciousness, in which object is created by it? Has the "nature" element no power of stimulation for the conscious side? We are familiar with the distinction of knowledge beginning in experience, but not originated by it. What has a writer like Mr Green to say on this point? This is quite a distinct alternative from any he puts. "Nature" may not originate knowledge; but it may be the occasion or commencement of it in such a sense that there would be no knowledge at all, but for it as a stimulus. Is this to be got over by the dictum that "understanding makes nature"? Would Mr Green have ventured to say that perception arises without a stimulus in consciousness from "nature" or the outward, whatever that be, whether an unconscious order, or a mind holding nature? And how, then, can he say that all nature, including this stimulus, is made by the consciousness or knowledge which it helps to make?

But is such an inference as that "consciousness" is not natural, or a result of nature, to be founded merely on a knowledge, real or supposed, of a process of change minus consciousness? Let us start from Hume's impressions, or series of impressions, each of which is supposed to be a consciousness. Here we have a process of change, or series of events, a series of consciousnesses. How is this series to be known by me? The consciousness attached to each impression will not give me knowledge of the series. It is restricted to each moment in the series. If the series is to be known by me, it must be known as one, with beginning, middle, and end, in time by me, conscious of each impression all through the process, and capable of combining these in the unity of the series. . Is the conscious act, in and through which I know the series, to be described as non-natural, or as otherwise than natural? Are the impressions to be regarded as "natural," while the conscious act of me the knower, is to be regarded as something other and higher than nature? Obviously this is a futile and misleading expression. It is perfectly true that the consciousness of the series is not the result of the series, is not the combined form of the separate consciousness, but a higher comprehension of the whole; but for this reason, to call it not natural is misleading. It is an essential part of the experience, and is as much "natural," in the proper sense of the word, as is the matter or impressions which it gathers into a single whole. It is a fact in time, continuous in time, and is, in a word, experience itself. It may very properly be called "a spiritual principle"; and this has a significance, if it be contrasted with either a real or conceived series of mere changes minus consciousness.

In fact, Hume himself, in the end, admitted the force of this criticism. In order to explain personal identity, he had recourse to memory, which recalls and gathers together our past perceptions, represents unceasingly their relations of resemblance and causality, and thus permits the imagination to pass easily from the one to the other, according to those principles of association, and to unite them all in an internal existence, unique and continuous. But, as he himself suggests, if "all our distinct perceptions are distinct existences," and if "the mind never perceives any real connection among distinct existences," how is this unifying of them, as in one consciousness, possible? That is the difficulty which he frankly acknowledges; and he further acknowledges that this difficulty is met by the supposition of our perceptions being inherent in something at once simple and individual. "Did our perceptions either inhere in something simple and individual, or did the mind perceive some real connection among them, there would be no difficulty in the case."[1] Hume, in fact, in this as on other points, provided both the bane and the antidote. If perceptions be so inherent, there is a possibility, nay, a necessity, of unifying them as in relation to one and the same individual consciousness; and this unity underlying all is sufficient to afford a real link of connection between perceptions that would be otherwise wholly distinct, as simply isolated impressions in isolated consciousnesses.

[1] *Treatise of Human Nature*, App., p. 636 (Selby-Bigge's edition).

III.—REALITY.

In order to reach those positions, we are offered by Mr Green a certain analysis of the conceptions "real" and "objective." It seems to amount to this, that there is an "impression" or "feeling,"—that we ask whether "an impression represents anything real and objective?" Of course, "some feeling must be felt" in order even to ask such a question. But the question means, "Whether a given feeling is what it is taken to be?—or, in other words, whether it is related as it seems to be related?" (p. 16.) Again, "Is a feeling, felt, really related as some one thinking about it takes it to be?" Then we have the illustration of the engine-driver, who "sees a signal wrong." It is not particularly illustrative; but it may be taken to mean that the engine-driver may think he sees a green light when it is red, and so drives on. The relations between the outward conditions of vision and the visual impression are real, as in normal vision; but the actual impression is *green*—viz., when it should have been *red* or, he thinks it *green*, when it is actually *red*. The driver mistakes the effect of one set of relations for that of another, and hence his error in vision. He should have seen red, but he actually saw, or thought he saw, green. But there is a permanent, or established, order here of relations—that is, between the determining or conditioning causes of vision and the actual but varying impressions. "A consciousness presents its experiences to itself as determined by relations, and, at the same time, conceives a simple and unalterable order of relations determining them, with which its temporary presentation . . . may be contrasted" (p. 17). The terms "real" and "objective" have a meaning only for such a consciousness.

But does this illustration not rather go against Mr Green's position? The signalman who, being colour-blind we may suppose, sees *green* when, according to the normal conditions of vision, he would have seen *red*, sees exactly what is real in the circumstances, and according to the conditions of his vision: nay, more, if every one's vision had been constituted as his, every one would have seen the *red* to be *green*. What, then, becomes of this illustration as proof that our sensations are only real as unalterably related to a certain set of conditions? It seems that in this case the impression was not real, because it was not in accordance with what a normally constituted vision would have seen or been impressed with. The truth is, the impression according to the circumstances or conditions of the colour-blind vision was, so far as this point goes, just as real as the other impression would have been to an ordinarily constituted eye. The true sense of the term *real* has already been lost. The reality of a sensation, perception, or conception is, in the first instance, just as it is to the mind; what it signifies or may be interpreted to mean in a sphere beyond itself is a wholly secondary point, and can only be a secondary form of reality.

The true conception of the real, according to this view, is to be sought for in a certain kind of relation between feelings, or between objects that we present to ourselves as sources of feeling. When we take the feelings rightly, or the relations rightly between those antecedents or concomitants, we have the real — the objective. This rightness is to be tested by the harmony between our "taking" the relation, or what some one thinking about it takes it to be, and "a single and unalterable order of relations determining the relations" in our consciousness.

(1.) The conception of the real or objective is presupposed in the very terms of such a statement. There can be no possible or actual agreement between a given relation or supposed relation of two feelings or facts in consciousness, without the presupposition that each feeling or fact is known to the conscious self as now, or as now and here—nay, is known as of a definite quality. A feeling is only as it *is* in time and consciousness. We have no conception of any feeling or impression which does not involve affirmation of its reality as now, or as now and here. And consequently, if reality consist in known relation, this relation cannot be merely of one feeling or fact to another, but of a feeling or fact to the conscious-subject; as little can it consist in the relation "between objects that we present to ourselves as sources of feeling."

But there is a confusion here all through between the interpretation of feelings or sensations and the reality of the sensations themselves. This latter is primary; the other is secondary, and to be inquired into through analogy and induction. Take the case of the relation between feeling and an object that is present as a source of feeling—that is, between feeling and feeling, for every object is ultimately a feeling conceived as related. I have before me the rose which I see, and I have in me, so to speak, the odour which I feel. The seeing the rose, or the impressions I have which make up the rose and the odour, are both present, and I relate the odour to the rose as its source—the feeling to the feeling. Now, and now only, have I any conception of reality or objectivity. If I misinterpret the feeling, and refer it to the rock on which grows the rose, then I have made a mistake as to the reality or true objectivity; but it is only in relation to this general conception of an objective unalterable order of relations between the feelings, that reality has a meaning for me. I have no other idea of reality than of correspondence between what seems to be related, and what is actually, absolutely, or unalterably related in an order of feelings. I say, in reply to this, that the odour I feel in presence of the rose is already real to me, whether I connect it with the rose or not as its source, whether I connect it with any feeling that went before it in consciousness; that it is not this kind of relation which, carried out, constitutes reality; that reality does not depend merely, or in the first instance, on my finding the true cause, much less relating the feeling to its place in an unalterable order, but on the simple presence of the feeling in my consciousness as felt, and occupying its place in time, and as doing so not necessarily in relation to any other feeling, but as a positive thing or quality known by me, and contrasted, it may be, with the absence of all other quality.

Further, the real or objective cannot consist simply in the relation or connection between one feeling and another, or a feeling and its source, however correctly known, for the reason that the feeling or fact is necessarily known as of this or that quality in the first instance, ere we can say anything about its relation to another feeling on the thread of consciousness, or of its relation to its source or cause. Quality grounds relation of kind. And though relation to time is indifferent to quality, the thing in time always has the mark of the *this now*, or *now and here*.

Nothing can be more absurd than the consequence of this doctrine, that we only reach the real—the truly real—when we do not blunder in the attempt to interpret the contents of our consciousness. If anything could make such a doctrine more ludicrous, it is the admission that in the process of mistake or failure, in the misinterpretation of the feeling, there is as much reality as in the successful relation of it to its source (p. 17). If there be as much reality here, how can the conception of the real be the harmony between related feelings and this objective determining order? How can reality mean a mistaken, unrealised relation, and a true correspondence with the unalterable order?

Mr Green proceeds to give us an account of the nature of the necessity of a conception, as distinct from the logical necessity of a conclusion contained in premisses conceded. This means that the conception is "necessary to the experience, without which there would not *for us be* a world at all, and there can be neither proof nor disproof of such necessity as is claimed for any conception, but through analysis of the conditions which render this experience possible" (p. 18).

This is the usual Kantian transcendental deduction, as now commonly interpreted. Given such or such an experience, consciousness, or knowledge of a world, this or that conception is necessary to the knowledge. Analyse such a knowledge, and you will find that the conception in question is implied in it. The (given or supposed) knowledge or experience is not possible without it. In this case, the distinction between facts and fancies implies "a conception of the world as a single system of relations." Idea of matter of fact, analysed, "means an idea of a relation which is always the same between the same objects." Again, "our idea of an object means that which is always the same in the same relations." "Each impression implies the idea of a world as a single and eternal system of related elements, which may be related with endless diversity, but must *be* related still."—(P. 19.)

Now, in the first place, the necessity of the conception here spoken of is a purely hypothetical necessity. If experience be so and so, a certain conception is necessary to its so being. Or as experience is identified with knowledge or a consciousness of objects, if this consciousness be as described, then this conception is necessary. But this experience, so described, must be shown or found to be as a matter of fact. It must be my actual experience as tested by psychological analysis. And the question is thus carried back to an earlier stage than that of the transcendental analysis or deduction. And this comes to be what precisely is the experience of which we are speaking. But let this be so; after all, a conception necessarily involved in it, so that it would not be the given experience or our experience, would be but an element of the possibility of this experience as conceived by us. It would not, in a word, be our experience, or experience for us, if we were to leave out one of its necessary elements. And what is this but a simple analysis of experience as we find it, tested by reflective analysis?

But, further, if the conception be thus involved, is it not involved in some other conception, which is part of the total experience or consciousness? It is not logically involved, we are told, as a conclusion in the premisses. These can be taken, comprehended, separately, and thereafter the conclusion may be or must be evolved. But if not in this way, in what way is the conception spoken of necessary? Is it necessary to the whole or complete act of experience? How shown—what is the process of "proof"? Obviously there is nothing in the shape of proof whatever under such conditions. If it be necessary to the total act of experience, if this be not possible, that is, conceivable without it, neither is the remanent part conceivable without this conception. We never, therefore, can start from the one to prove the other, or draw the other, for the two or more elements are given us necessarily together in the complex act. If, for example, a self-distinguishing consciousness be necessary to a conscious relation, we never can conceive the one apart from the other, and so evolve the other out of it, for the simple reason, that neither is conceivable apart. All that we can say is, that we find this in experience. It is further to be noted that this analysis amounts to no more than an analysis of knowledge, or experience as known, as consciousness. It does not touch in any way the question how this experience, as a matter of fact, has actually arisen. Yet these two points of view are confounded all through the discussion; for we hear quietly, as if it were quite the same thing, "of the necessary character of the ideas which it [the analysis] exhibits as operative in the formation of experience" (p. 18); whereas it is but the analysis of the ideas which already make up this very experience which is possible in the case, and which, when we try to think them apart, we cannot succeed. In other words, we fall back on a necessity test simply by reflective analysis.

As to this argument from "the transcendental proof," so much vaunted, and so variously stated, little need be said at this point. Even if it were valid, it does not bear on the implication of a universal self in the individual self of time. This is asserted to be a necessary inference, because the denial of it would involve all our experience in contradiction (p. 258). I have never seen anything of the slightest force in the way of supplying a link between premiss and conclusion here. It seems to me even, on the other hand, that the assertion of such an entity involves the whole of our experience in contradiction. It is an express contradiction to assert an individual ego in time, much more a plurality of such egos, along with one universal ego which must necessarily absorb all — be all and every one. And it is to introduce into human knowledge an element of fundamental uncertainty, when we are represented as first accepting the individual ego for the individual which it alleges itself to be in time and consciousness, and then finding out in the end that it is no such thing, but the universal ego struggling with the hostile conditions of the animal organism.

The analysis of "the idea of a matter of fact" as "an idea of a relation which is always the same between the same objects"—and of "the idea of an object as that which is always the same in the same relations," is about as remarkable an example of tautological verbalism as could well be found. How could a relation be different "between the same objects," or how could an object be otherwise than "the same in the same relations"? Is not, further, relation here secondary —dependent on the same objects? And how do we know that two objects in different times are the same? Would this not be a knowledge prior to the relation? And how could two objects be the same object? How could they be anything but similar? The relation would thus be founded on something prior to it—that is, quality and even likeness in quality.

But the point to be kept in view, towards which all these statements are meant to tend, is, that our experience or consciousness of objects cannot arise out of a series of objects of which there is no consciousness, either ours or some other. "A consciousness of events as a related series— experience in the most elementary form in which it can be the beginning of knowledge—has not any element of identity with, and therefore cannot properly be said 'to be developed out of a mere series of related events,' of successive modifications of body or soul, such as is experience in the former of the senses spoken of. No one, and no number of a series of related events, can be the consciousness of the series as related. Nor can any product of the series be either. . . . A consciousness of certain events cannot be anything that thus succeeds them. It must be equally present to all the events of which it is the consciousness. For this reason an intelligent experience, or experience as the source of knowledge, can neither be constituted by events of which it is the experience, nor be a product of them."—(P. 21.)

"Experience has two meanings—simply change, and the consciousness of change. There is a series of changes—chemical or atmospheric—in the growth of the plant. There is the definite physical experience of changes in sleep. But this is different from the experience which is a knowledge of nature or the consciousness of change."—(P. 20.)

Now the main position here is eminently sound—that is, that a consciousness of a series of events is not possible as a part of the mere series of events, or as the product of it. The consciousness, or, much better, the permanent conscious subject, must be present to each of the events in the series, otherwise the series cannot be known as a series, or in fact at all. But there is, as usual, a change of terms in the conclusion drawn from this. The writer no longer there speaks of the conscious experience merely as the intelligent experience of the series, but experience " as the source of knowledge "; and thus doubles, so to speak, the expression, with a view to show that conscious experience is not only to be distinguished from a mere series of related events, but is that from which knowledge itself—that is, the conscious experience—springs. And this fallacious mode of statement is emphasised by distinguishing further the events of which it is the experience, and so doubly, even trebly, confounding the meaning of words. If experience—

that is, conscious experience—be not a mere unconscious series of events, neither can it be said to have an intelligent experience as a source of knowledge—that is, a source of itself, or knowledge as a source of knowledge.

But there is another point here. It may be true that a consciousness of related events cannot spring from a mere series of related events; it does not follow that the knowledge or consciousness of the series is constituted simply by "a consciousness which is equally present to all the events of which it is the consciousness" (p. 21). A consciousness thus present in succession to each event can only be an act of consciousness—an intuition of each event in succession, and therefore, in each a different intuition in time, varying numerically with the event. Such "a consciousness" is utterly inadequate to give us "a consciousness of the series." We do not thus advance one whit beyond Hume's doctrine of conscious impressions. What is needed for the consciousness of a series is not simply a consciousness present to each, but a permanent conscious or knowing subject putting forth a conscious act in the successive times, and, in virtue of its own identity, gathering up the acts in one common conception as those of a series. Thus is the knowledge or experience by us of the series constituted, but it does not follow that the series is constituted by the permanent identical conscious subject. There must be in the series, as grounding the knowledge of it, a feature or condition independent, in the first place, of the knowing act, which enables the subject to differentiate it from what is not a series, but, say, a coexistence of events or the relation of causality. These are as truly relations as that of succession, though of quite a different character.

But are we left to the alternatives, as is here assumed, of consciousness arising from a series of unconscious events, and that of consciousness arising from a prior or primary consciousness of events? The impossibility of the former may be established. Are we necessarily driven to the alternative of derivation of our consciousness from a prior or primary consciousness of a series of events? By no means. May not our consciousness be as a power to be developed into act or reality, in and along with the concurring series of events? Is there anything impossible or improbable even in there being, as contemporaneous entities, time-conscious acts and time-succeeding things? Is the existence of a subject in time capable of rising to consciousness under certain conditions, and thus a real entity in time, less reasonable as a conception than "a consciousness equally present to all the events of which it is the consciousness"? Nay, does not the latter supposition involve the conception first of a capable conscious subject enduring in time? Does the conception of a primary consciousness of events, above time apparently, from which our time-consciousness is supposed to arise, help us to connect with its cause—that is, explain the rise of our time-consciousness—any more than the mere series of related events?

But we are further told that "any consciousness of change, since the whole of it must be present at once, cannot be itself a process of change. There may be a change into a state of consciousness of change, and a change out of it, on the part of this man or that; but within the consciousness itself there can be no change, because no relation of before and after, of here and there, between its constituent members—between the presentation, for instance, of point A and that of point B in the process which forms the object of consciousness."—(P. 22.)

We have here a process of change—the presentation of point A, then of point B, necessarily in succession. This process in succession is the object of consciousness; one consciousness must be present to each point, in order to be conscious of the change; but there can be no change in the consciousness itself which knows the change,—no relation of before and after, of here and there, between its constituent members, "since the whole of it must be present at once." There is here a contradiction, a simple absurdity. In or through one single immovable consciousness there pass conscious points A and B—that is, conscious acts directed in succession to objects—yet there is no change in the consciousness. The consciousness knows the process of change, but it itself suffers no change—admits of no change or modification whatever—"since the whole of it must be present at once." If there be a consciousness or knowledge of a definite change in things—of a succession of objects in a definite time — there must be a corresponding change in the series of cognitive or conscious acts, otherwise the conception of the process would be impossible. This conception of the completed process as one of change is, no doubt, one and indivisible; but it is a conception all the same which is possible only through the grouping in one of changes consciously known in the series. The unity and identity here is not of the consciousness itself, but of the conscious subject, existing through the series, and putting forth definite conscious acts in succession, and in the end setting forth its conception of the process as one of change. There is here the usual confusion between consciousness and the conscious subject, — the confusion between consciousness as a mere abstraction or term and the definite acts of consciousness which make it up.

The understanding, accordingly, enables us to conceive that there is such a thing as the order of nature—that is, "certain relations regarded as forming a single system;" and further, the understanding "which presents an order of nature to us, is in principle one with an understanding which constitutes that order itself" (p. 23). The conception opposed to this is that of an order of nature on the one side and the conception of an order of nature on the other, and between them "some unaccountable pre-established harmony."

Here Locke is taken as the representative of "the traditional philosophy of common sense." There can hardly be clearer evidence of the lack of knowledge in the history of modern philosophy than such a statement. "The philosophy of common sense," as represented by Reid and Hamilton, is a wholly different thing in conception from any view of Locke, especially any view of his regarding sensation and perception. Locke expressly held that there is no direct or immediate apprehension of an external world — the world of things. There is, in his view, (1) sensation—

as of sound, colour, taste, smell, &c. But sensation is not a quality of things; it is simply a state of the mind, caused by things to which it has no resemblance, and whose nature, therefore, it does not convey to us. There is, (2) "the idea," or ideas, in perception. These are real resemblances of certain qualities inseparable from matter, as extension, solidity, figure, mobility.

Hamilton, on the other hand, expressly, and Reid in all probability, held an intuitive or immediate apprehension of the quality of the material world as present to, and existing for, consciousness; and they maintain that this view is in accordance with universal belief, while that of Locke is distinctly opposed to it. As to the ground of the first principles of knowledge—the philosophy of common sense proper—they do not differ less from Locke, though here what is called "intellectualism" in Locke is to be considered. If there is one point more than another which Reid contests, and contests successfully, in his Second and Sixth Essays, it is the fundamental position of Locke's philosophy, that knowledge consists in "the perception of the connection and agreement, or disagreement and repugnance, of any of our ideas;" and not less strenuously does he contend that the hypothesis of "ideas" in perception cannot give the slightest knowledge of the real world. This constant persistent misrepresentation of what they are pleased to term "common sense" is a characteristic of Neo-Kantian writers down to the present moment.

But Locke, it appears, holds sensation to be real because we cannot make it, and relations not to be real because we make them—because they are the work of the mind. What is said in reply to this is certainly remarkable in itself and its broad assumptiveness. "Without relation," we are told, "any simple idea would be undistinguished from other simple ideas, undetermined by its surroundings in the cosmos of experience. It would thus be unqualified."—(P. 23.) In other words, no sensation or quality of matter can be to us an object of consciousness, unless as some other simple sensation or idea known to us determines it, qualifies it, as of this or that sort. No single colour can be known unless we know another colour, or it may be a taste, an odour, or a sound. But is there not the same difficulty in regard to knowing the other simple sensation or quality which there is in regard to the first, as yet undistinguished and undetermined? How are we to know the other or surrounding simple sensation or quality, if we do not already know that which it surrounds? How can we speak of another quality at all in such a connection, when as yet there is not one to begin with,—it waiting all the while on its surroundings to be determined to be, while this is equally waiting on its neighbour? What does this, in fact, logically carried out, imply, but that we cannot know anything because we cannot know everything?

The mistake here, and it is a vital one, running through the whole reasoning of those chapters, is the making that primary—viz., relation, which is only secondary; substituting for the quality, even the reality, of a thing, that which can only be founded on it. Besides, there is a confusion of two quite different kinds of relation—the relations of objects to each other, metaphysical and physical, and the relation of the known object to the knowing subject,—a confusion, in fact, between the relations among existing things and the relations of the knower to the known existing world.

In ordinary thinking, it is said, we oppose the work of the mind to the real, not as the work of the mind, as such, but the work of the mind as assumed to be arbitrary and irregularly changeable (p. 25). But it seems that the question—What is the real?—which we seek to answer by means of this opposition is "a misleading one, so far as it implies the self-contradictory supposition of there really being something other than the real from which it could be distinguished" (p. 29). But apparently we may ask and decide the question, "Whether any particular event or object is really what it seems to be, or whether our belief about it is true?" And the test of this is, "the unalterableness of the qualities which we ascribe to it, or which form its apparent nature" (p. 27). "Whatever anything is really, it is unalterably." "A sensation is the unalterable effect of its conditions, whatever those conditions may be." "The unalterableness of the fact that a certain feeling is felt under certain conditions, is ascribed to the simple feeling."—(Pp. 27, 28.)

"The inquiry into the real is as to an unchanging relation between the appearance and its conditions, or an unchanging relation between these and certain other conditions."—(P. 29.) "That there *is* an unalterable order of relations, if we could only find it out, is the presupposition of all our inquiry into the real nature of appearances; and such unalterableness implies their inclusion in one system which leaves nothing outside itself."—(P. 30.)

We cannot answer the question, What is the real? because the real is everything. There is nothing that is unreal. There is not reality and non-reality. We may make a judgment about the real which is false. We may form an erroneous opinion. "The relations by which, in a false belief as to a matter of fact, we suppose the event to be determined, are not non-existent. They are really objects of a conceiving consciousness. As arising out of the action of such a consciousness, as constituents of a world which it presents to itself, they are no less real than are the actual conditions of the event which is thought to be, but is not really determined by them."—(P. 26.) It is hardly necessary, as seems to me, to go further than this for the *reductio ad absurdum* of the philosophical system of which it is the teaching. Subjective illusion, error, false judgment about facts and the order of things, are real, equally real, with the knowledge of objective truth—with true judgment about facts and the order of facts—because both are equally relations in the mind or consciousness, and perhaps the work of the mind. These relations are not non-existent, therefore they are real, equally real, with the true relations also determined by the mind. Whatever the mind determines, whether it represents correctly an object and its conditions or not, is equally real. We cannot, therefore, say a fact falsely alleged—viz., the death of a person—is unreal; for although it is a false judgment, it is still a judgment, and therefore not unreal. Was there ever such a confusion in the application of the word *real?* Cannot we get a test of the real in its application, say, to matter of fact in general, so as thus to distinguish what is, as a matter of fact, from what we may think to be, but which never was, nor will be? Is it the same kind of reality of which we are speaking when we say this event did not happen, and I erroneously judge that this event did happen? The whole plausibility of this reasoning, if it deserves the name, is the confusion between the subjective individual judgment or thought about reality, and the objective reality of the fact itself—of existence itself. These are not both equally real; they are not real in the same sense. There is not an opposition between the happening of the fact and my erroneous judgment about it, but between the happening and the non-happening of the fact. What is the real in matter of fact is a perfectly competent question, and we can answer this question so as to say this is real, that is unreal. We are dealing in the first instance, in both cases, with our conceptions or thoughts about the real; but the real does not lie in the mere representation of the fact, but in the fact itself as standing to us in a correct representation. "The real is everything," is about as weak and unanalysed a statement as could well be made. The real is thus what is and what is not—what occurred and what did not occur—what we perceive and what we imagine—what we see and what we dream—what is true and what is false; and it is all this equally, simply forsooth because these are things or relations in consciousness! All the blunderings of individuals during the past striving to represent the course of things in science, have been equally real with the true representation, and on the same level as the real order of nature itself.

But these strivings and blunderings in the individual mind to get at the true relations of things —what are they? Are they the workings of an individual subject or consciousness, different from the absolute or eternal consciousness, which holds everything in being? Then he too—this individual subject—must be real as the eternal consciousness is real, for he too is—is, in fact, our consciousness. Then there will be two realities, coequal, not one simply, as we are told, with a double aspect. Are these blunderings the blunderings of the Eternal Consciousness, omniscient and omnipotent—the all-creator, the all-sustainer? But how can this power blunder, or be anything but what he is — absolute and eternal truth? The admission points to the central weakness of the system. "The eternal consciousness" is a name simply for what we know and realise of consciousness — that is, our own; sufficiently blundering and progressive, but confessedly never complete.

Suppose we substitute " the true " for " the real," —are we to dismiss this question as to what is the true, because this supposes that there is something untrue? But if not, why not? Why dismiss the question of the real on this ground, and not that of the true? Does not asking the question, what is the true, suppose or imply that there may be something which is untrue? But can there be anything untrue to my consciousness, if my consciousness always presents to me relations of things when it presents the true, and relations of things when it presents the untrue? Not certainly unless there be a test of true and of untrue relations. But if reality consist in relation, how can there be both true and untrue relations in my consciousness? My relation is for the moment just what it is, and nothing more. Am I then to seek another relation which will correct this present relation? But this other relation is only itself a relation in my consciousness; and if I have nothing but relation as a test of relation, why should I reasonably prefer the one to the other, or say the one relation is true and the other not? I am just as much precluded, on the grounds set forth, from asking the question, What is the true? as from asking the question, What is the real?

But we are now confronted after all this with a singular admission. Though we cannot ask the question, What is the real? we can ask the question, What is the real in particular events? whether any particular event is really what it seems to be? whether our belief about it is real? And we can settle this question. We can get a test of it—the test, namely, of unalterableness between sensation and its conditions, and between these conditious and other conditions. But surely if we can determine the real in particular events, as, say, an unchanging relation between the appearance and its conditions, how can it be said that the question, What is the real, is meaningless? Is this not saying that the real means, or is an unchanging relation between, two terms? We are told even that this is "the essence of reality." How, then, is it impossible for us even to put the question? Does the writer actually suppose that in asking what is the real, we are not dealing with it in particular cases, and in its various applications? or that our answer would be anything but a generalised test in the different classes of cases, or if possible a universal test for all individual instances? But what of the consistency with his own position? If the real in a particular case be the unalterableness of a given sensation and its conditions, will not the unreal be the mistaken judgment we make about this sensation and its conditions? Will it not be that we have judged that the thing seems to be so and so, while it is not? But what becomes of the statement made a little ago, that anything into which relation for consciousness enters is real—nay, equally real,— that there is no unreal at all?

Truth, in Mr Green's view, consists in a feeling being related by us as it is actually related in the order of the world—that is, in the Eternal Consciousness. He admits that we may and do blunder about the true relations. Even this should be a puzzle for his system, since it is the Eternal Consciousness which is manifesting itself in relations through us, and yet there is a possibility—nay, an actuality—of mistake as to the true import of our knowledge, and the real place of feelings in the one unalterable related order. But the fatal flaw in the Eternal Consciousness as a standard of objectivity, with which we have to compare our conceptions of order and connection, is that we do not know it as an independent standard at all. It is only partially revealed in us,—as far as our animal organism will permit. Though in us, we are not it, and therefore cannot know it as it is. It is God alone, as Mr Green tells us, who can know

God, and therefore know the world. The partial revelation is all we know. All is but a manifestation in us of an otherwise hidden Eternal Spirit or order of relations. We know but in part; we know what is vouchsafed to us; but we are not in a position to compare our conceptions of the relations with the relations as in reality—as in the Eternal Consciousness. We are thus left in utter uncertainty as to whether our thoughts do correspond with the thought-relations that make up the universe. Truth thus ceases to be capable of being conceived as a harmony between thought and things. We have not, as on the ordinary view, presentations of sense on the one hand and representations or thoughts of these on the other. We have simply a series of thoughts or thought-relations succeeding each other—one coming, then passing, and being replaced by another. Past, present, and future would be simply a stream of thoughts. Could we on such a scheme preserve even self-consistency or non-contradictoriness in our thoughts? There is nothing in the mere sequence of thoughts to keep them consistent with each other. There is no reason why negation should not directly follow affirmation, and the thought which affirmed should be succeeded by the thought which denied the same thing. But as thought-relation of the moment, incapable of being related to any objective standard, there is not the slightest test of the truth of our thoughts, or power of deciding between the affirmation and the negation of the subject to which they relate. Here we come back pretty well, notwithstanding the absolutist pretensions, to the *Homo mensura* of Protagoras, and the mere flow of subjective impressions. Truth and certainty have no longer any real meaning in knowledge.

It is clear, I think, that Mr Green has not analysed the connotation of the real, nor has he properly considered its various applications. To restrict the real to " an unchanging relation between the appearance and its conditions, or an unchanging relation between these and certain other conditions," is simply to put a part for the whole, and to leave out meanings of the real without which such a relation could not even be conceived. In its primary application the *real* means something apprehended as existing, in opposition to that which is not so apprehended, or in opposition to the absence of any appearance whatever. In the earliest conceivable form of Perception there is something apprehended—not nothing; and we mean by the real at first the appearance, percept, impression, whatever we come to call it, which is known to consciousness, as opposed to the blank or negation of it. Impression and no impression, at a given time, cannot be identified. We call the impression *real;* we speak of the absence of impression as the *unreal.* We cannot identify these, unless on pain of the total subversion of knowledge and rationality. The impression or percept may be perceived, and its absence may be thought by us, but this does not identify them, or make them both real in any true or equal sense of the term. This is the real for us—existence known or apprehended by us, as opposed to what is conceived, it may be, but ideal only; the negation or opposite, but properly unreal. Unless this form of reality is given or apprehended by us, we are powerless to think even of its relations to anything whatever, before or after it. So far as this form of reality is conceived, there can hardly be any mistake about it. It exists for consciousness—it exists while I am conscious of it; and accordingly it is exactly what I am conscious it is—what I feel to be, or what I know to be. The sensation I experience can only be the sensation of the moment; the percept I have can only be the percept of the moment. I affirm it to be, implicitly or explicitly, and it can only be as I affirm it. It exists as in consciousness. I may, no doubt, proceed further, and affirm that it is related to something that went before it, that it will be related to something that comes after it, that it is related to something which accompanies; but here I enter on a new sphere altogether. I go beyond my actual consciousness, and judge apart how it stands either to other actual states of consciousness, or to possible states of consciousness, or to conditions of states of consciousness. And here I may very readily go wrong—judge wrongly as to its real relations; but the reality of the sensation, percept, or concept, as for me a conscious object, stands untouched. And I commit a very grave blunder if I confound the truth of the relation which I make or affirm with the reality of the object in my consciousness, or the untruth of the relation which I affirm, with the unreality which would be identical with the absence of the object, sensation, or percept from my consciousness.

There are, besides, other meanings of the term *real*. It not only means what is, as for consciousness now, or now and here; it means also what is supposed to be, whether it is an actual object of consciousness or not. Unless we suppose what we call the outward world to be simply a series of revelations to the individual or individuals of the race, successively inspired in them—in fact, created in each succeeding moment of perception—we must suppose some continuity in that world and in its related parts. There are not only actual percepts, there are possible percepts for each individual—nay, for the whole individuals of mankind, for science is not yet exhausted. And we may, and do, apply the term reality to the possible new knowledge which is thus open to us, or rather to that supposed continuous source of this knowledge. And it matters nothing at present whether we regard this outward world as a material force or as an abiding mind. This we hold to be *real*, as the continuous source to us of sensations and perceptions which we do not create. This is, properly speaking, *objective reality*—objective reality in the proper and characteristic sense of the term. It is reality outside of our consciousness, not for us an actual object of consciousness. And no one has a right to discuss reality, as simply meaning relation or relations among even known objects, without expressly considering it in this its objective, it may be supersensible, aspect.

There is the distinction actually accepted in philosophy, actually proceeded upon in all our thinking, of the real as existing for our consciousness and as we are conscious of it, and the real as having an existence in its own nature somehow for itself. In the widest sense of the term, *real* embraces both forms of existence, though the latter, as not actually apprehended in consciousness, but only conceived by us, may fairly be regarded from our point of view as *ideal*.

Further, there is still a third application of the term *real*. It applies not only to what is—to what is actually realised, but it is used for what may and ought to be. In some departments of knowledge we are able to sketch beforehand—to outline what we call the true reality, as opposed to the imperfect or unrealised. We are even able in some cases to say this ought to be, when it is not. It is so in all ethical precepts, and in all laws relating to imaginative construction. We can depict the ideal of moral character, though it does not exist; and the perfect form in imagination, though we do not find it in fact. This we say is the real, not the imperfect, development. This is properly the reality of the type; and here, as the type is not as yet realised, the real coincides with the ideal.

Recently certain writers, who may fairly enough be classed as Neo-Kantian, have essayed to meet objections to certain of the points now indicated, while modifying often materially the common positions of Hegel and Green. The two main points referred to are—(1) that reality is only "for knowledge"; and (2) the doctrine that the individual is alone real.

(1.) The former point touches the essence of the whole controversy. What is, is for knowledge— is the thesis. But it does not seem to me to be cleared in the discussion, or made more certain.

When I am told that there is "no outside of consciousness which has really any meaning," and when I am told at the same time that the individual self or consciousness of space and time is not that consciousness which makes experience possible, I confess I am puzzled to know what answer is meant to be given to the question as to the extension of the term reality—as to what is meant to be called real—and, much more, as to the permanency of the real and its ground. Reality is obviously held to be more than my experience or that of any individual whatever. It is not allowed to be an element foreign to thought or consciousness on which it may work. It is not properly something existing, in space and time, apart from me, the conscious subject, for this would be to put it "outside of consciousness," and outside of consciousness has no meaning. I am not even allowed to postulate an absolute thought or consciousness, in which this reality is to abide. It is neither outside of my consciousness, nor is it inside another consciousness—at least, an absolute or supreme consciousness. Then what is the explanation of its being more than my conscious impression, as Hume puts it, or the conscious impression of some individual who would necessarily be "outside my consciousness," and therefore meaningless, quite as much as any "foreign element"? For nothing can be more foreign to me than an other self. This implies absolute exclusion,—exclusion in space, time, and conception, in reality and in thought.

But the refuge seems to be that all reality is "for knowledge": what is the meaning of this phrase? Is "knowledge" here used as an abstraction—as a simple term or conception? How can all reality be said to be for this? The conception of knowledge and the fact of knowing are utterly different things. The "knowledge" spoken of must be the act of some subject or person. But it is not the act of me, the individual of time and space, for reality is much wider than any knowledge of mine; and it is as little completed in all the individuals of the race. Then there is on this view of the doctrine no absolute ego or intelligence for whose knowledge anything is. In what sense, then, can complete reality be "for knowledge"? The answer seems to be given in the statement, "that thought does not, as we find it in our experience, exhaust the predicates of the subject or its judgments, or present those contents in the form of individual existence here and now."[1] In other words, our thought is capable of indefinite progression, though it never can rise above a relational knowledge, never can actually complete knowledge. How this should constitute the difference between thought and fact, it is hard to see. Because thought never can complete the knowledge of fact, thought is different from fact. I should have imagined that if thought knows fact, and yet cannot complete its knowledge of it, that thought and fact were already different in the first act of knowledge; and if so, that the difference cannot depend quite on the circumstance of the inadequacy of thought bound to relations to complete knowledge, and so transcend itself.

This is advanced to meet the question as to "the nature of the reality which there is in the object of knowledge, over and above ordinary knowledge itself."[2] It seems a somewhat odd solution of the problem. It may amount simply to saying that relational knowledge is capable of endless progress, but how this throws light on "the nature of reality over and above ordinary knowledge," is not clear. Nor is there the

[1] *Mind*, No. LII., p. 588.   [2] *Ibid.*, p. 587.

slightest connection between the two statements. Or it may be taken as implying that there is reality beyond ordinary knowledge which we, bound as we are in relations, cannot definitely grasp. This seems to be the meaning of sentences such as these: "It is this completion of thought beyond thought which remains for ever an Other. Thought can form the idea of an apprehension, something like feeling in its directness, which contains all the features desired by its relational efforts. It can understand that, in order to attain to this goal, it must get beyond relations. Yet it can find in its nature no other way of progress. . . . It perceives that this essential side of its nature must somehow be merged, so as to take in the other side. But such a fusion would force it to transcend its present self — how in vague generality it does apprehend, but how in detail it cannot understand, and it can see the reason why it cannot. This self-transcendence *is* an Other, but to assert it is *not* a self-contradiction."[1]

This impossibility, then, of definite knowledge on our part — this impossibility of actual self-transcendence — constitutes "the nature of the reality which there is in the object of knowledge over and above ordinary knowledge itself." It

[1] *Mind*, No. LII., p. 589.

seems to me to amount to little more than saying that if we seek to transcend our ordinary or relational knowledge, we shall fail to reach any definite conception, though we have a conviction that there is something called an Other, which we do not and never can grasp. How this incapacity on our part throws any light on the nature of reality beyond ordinary knowledge, or anywhere else, is to me an absolute puzzle. I should venture even to think that if we knew a thing only as we do not know it, we should not know it at all. Yet this is cited as the essence of Neo-Kantianism as it now is, and the great and precious legacy which it has received from Hegelianism—otherwise not of much value.

But the admission here, that reality must always come to us in relation and relational knowledge, is an important one. This transcendent Other is known to be—that is all. It is for our knowledge. It is an Other to that knowledge. It is the dark shadow of our actual knowledge, which, like the moon with its bright and dark side, is utterly non-infusible. But is this the correct inference from the fact of the relativity of knowledge? Reality in its widest extent is confessedly beyond us, wider than we; it is ever appearing in knowledge, but never there completed. Does this not imply that reality, as it appears for our knowledge, is but a part of what actually is—symbol or manifestation it may be; that along with our definite relational knowledge of fact we have a conception of reality, indefinite it may be, but still a conception of existence as transcending our knowledge of details or characters; and although we may always have to shape our definite knowledge in relations—to refer it to time, space, and category—these are inadequate to the full sphere of being as it actually is at the moment of our knowledge? Let us admit that reality must always come to us in relation, or as known be "for knowledge,"—this does not prove that reality only is as it is in relation or "for knowledge." It may be wrong, it is true, that the very being "for knowledge" implies the being not "for knowledge," if by "knowledge" we mean our definite relational knowledge. For this being for knowledge needs a ground; and if there be no ground outside of our definite acts of knowledge, then these successive acts are simply the spontaneous creations of facts themselves—in a word, of the universe — and thus we land in simple Egoism.

(2.) If we run back the reality of the physical world to its furthest point, on what may be called its material as opposed to its formal side, we shall reach the atom. This may be taken as the individually real, and the ground of aggregate individual reality in the time and space we know. To this it has been said, by way of criticism, that an atom is "a category" by which we make the world intelligible to ourselves, and that "if the reality of things consists in their being composed of atoms, then it follows that their reality consists in their being thought."[1]

This of course implies the wide proposition, that whatever we think as the constituent of the universe, be it atom, monad, or force of any sort, is real only because we think it, or at least because it is thought by some one; because, in a word, it is necessarily an object of thought. Thus the thinking a thing or object makes its reality. When we understand how a thing is done, the understanding is the mode of the doing of the thing, and there is no reality in the mode of doing, but only in our thinking the mode of doing. From this it follows, first, that as our thinking the mode is a process now, and there is no reality but in the thinking of the process, the world, in this case, is constituted for the first time along with the thinking, in the thinking, and consequently the constitution of the reality of the universe was not a thing of the past, but of the present—nay, is the thought of the thinker

[1] *Mind*, No. L., April 1888, p. 256 *et seq.*

who understands it. If this thought be the act of the individual thinker of time and space, then the reality of the constitution of the universe, and with it that of the universe itself, comes and goes with the thought of the individual consciousness. If the "thought" spoken of be an abstraction from the individual altogether, it has either no meaning, or it is the thought of something called an eternal or absolute consciousness, which cannot be shown to have the slightest connection with the world of time and space. Such a theory, therefore, affords no explanation whatever of the past genesis of the universe, or of the permanent continuance of that universe. But the truth is, that the statement of the identity of reality and thought, or known reality, is simply an assumption of the whole point at issue, and an illustration of the pervading fallacy of Hegelian method.

To the statement that the individual alone is real, it has been objected that we cannot know any individual except in its universal aspect—that "the individual is unknown just in so far as we cannot universalise it." The "universal" is not merely a sum of individuals. The individual apart from the universal is as much an abstraction as the universal apart from the individual. The individual is consequently not more real than the universal.

It is perfectly true that for us there is no conception of an individual *per se*. This we may allow to be an abstraction—in fact, worse, it is an impossibility in our thinking. The furthest back we can go in thinking the individual, we have yet to think it in *being*, as *one*, as in *time*, as *this* not *that*. Difference and relation necessarily enter into every conception of the ultimate in individuality. This is so. But does it follow from this that the universal feature in the individual—in the *this* or *that* of experience—is equally real with the *this* or *that* which we actually perceive or apprehend? If we conceive an individual simply—say, an equilateral triangle—the individual image which we frame may fairly enough be regarded as on the same level of reality with the universals embodied in it, with three-sidedness and equilateralness; but is the triangular object which I apprehend as here and now before me in space and time, to be treated exactly as my concept of the ideal triangle is? It is perfectly clear, as seems to me, that to any one not blinded by baseless philosophical assumptions, there is a whole world of difference in the two cases. It may quite well be that we cannot state specifically the elements of difference, at least fully; but that a difference there is, and that in this difference lies precisely the nature of reality, there can, I think, be no question for any one who is faithful to the teaching of experience. The universal which I recognise in the individual is not that which constitutes the individual, for the simple reason that it equally constitutes any other individual of the type, and by this conflicts with the very notion of individuality. So far from its being true that we cannot know the individual except in its universal aspect, it is true that the individual so known or so regarded is no longer individual—is simply merged in the generic type.

This inseparable correlation of the individual and the universal is used in the so-called proof or establishment of the universal self. This is maintained to be, and to be the real—in fact, ultimately the only real self—against the view that the individual self of time is the true real, and the universal self a mere abstraction. But if the principle fails in a lower sphere, it fails here above all. The fact of the individuality of the self of time and consciousness in no way implies the reality of a self above time and consciousness, which is supposed to be the "condition" of both. There is in the first place a confusion here between a self—a real existing self—and self-hood. The individual self of time certainly implies the conception—call it a universal—of self-hood; and this may be shared in by other individuals in time, real or possible. But this mere self-hood is not a self in the sense of the individual of time and consciousness. And it is most illegitimately set up as a real self, called Eternal or Universal, in correlation with the self of time. There is no such correlate or implicate in the conception of the self of time. There is the element—the possibly universal element—of self-hood or selfness; but this has no title to be regarded as a self above time, or as anything but what it is—a simple abstraction.

IV.—RELATION.

WE come now to the question of the nature of Relation. On this mainly depends the answer to the question: Whether the all-inclusive principle of an Eternal Self-consciousness is needed to constitute the system of things or relations?

On the subject of relation generally, I do not find in Mr Green's statement anything like an adequate discrimination between what may be regarded as the two fundamental forms of relation—viz., (1) the relation between the knower, consciousness or conscious subject, and the object known; and (2) the relation between or among objects known—that is, in respect of each other. The former may be called subjective relativity; the latter objective. I do not find this essential distinction recognised explicitly by Mr Green, and I find very constantly in his reasoning a confusion of these, the two forms of relation. Indeed he seems to use the phrase " related to consciousness" as synonymous with "knowledge of phænomena," and also with "the correlation of subject and object." But the relations between phænomena considered as matter of knowledge, and the relation, constant and permanent, between the conscious subject and the object, are not to be lightly assumed as of the same character; nor are they so in point of fact. Even supposing it were shown that knowledge of a phænomenon necessarily implies the knowledge of its relation to another phænomenon,— that it is given, or found only in, some such relationship,—this would not prove that the kind of relationship thus found is of the same nature as the relationship between the conscious knower and the related thing known. The latter relationship, while universal, necessary, may be wholly unique in kind. Knowledge, as a general fact, arises when conscious subject and object are together or correlated in time; but it will not be pretended that the one term—the conscious subject—is always or necessarily of the same nature as the object with which it is in correlation. It will not be pretended surely that the space-object which we know—call it relation or anything you choose—is of the same nature as the conscious subject or consciousness which knows it. It will surely not be pretended even that the coloured surface is of the same nature as the perceiving subject of consciousness. The knower or perceiver is certainly different in character from extension, solidity, incompressibility in bodies, from mechanical, chemical, and other forces, which yet it apprehends or knows. If this be so, the relationship of knowledge which arises from the correlation of the subject and object is of quite a different kind from the relationship subsisting among those objects themselves as space-objects. It will not be pretended that they are in respect of each other of an essentially different nature. They are distinctly homogeneous; and accordingly a relation between them as homogeneous things is a wholly different kind of relation from that of knowledge between the subject knowing and the object known. There does not appear to be any apprehension of this distinction throughout Mr Green's discussion; and the result is, that a conclusion thus depending on the wholly ambiguous premiss of "related to consciousness" is of very little value. If we look only to the sphere of objective relationship, we may find things so actually interlaced in their details that they cannot be apprehended or known by us out of mutual connection. If we look to the sphere of the subject and object, in its essential relationship, we may find no such fixed or necessary connection as that the particulars or particular objects known are unalterably related to it, or even unalterably related to it in any given case. The subject may be wholly free to deal with object or objects, though it is always connected with *some* object. It may quite well have a place or standing of its own amid all objects, and yet be necessarily related to none; while in the objective sphere the homogeneous phænomena appear to us actually inseparable. So far as the conscious subject is concerned, these may appear to be inseparable, unalterable at least by it. And yet it—the subject itself—may remain independent amid the flow and variety of the details, whose relationship to each other is wholly unlike its own relationship to any.

By this confusion we illegitimately anticipate conclusions on the vital questions of philosophy. Let us suppose that the objective phænomena are related through the law of physical causality,—through the law of the transformation and transmutation of energy. This may be considered apart from the question of the necessity or unalterableness of the relation. Are we at once to assume that the relation of subject and object is so regulated?—that object is simply the energy of the subject transformed into an opposite to itself? But if we identify the objective, and, so to speak, subjective relationships, how are we to escape this conclusion?

We need hardly pursue this matter into its details. But surely it will be admitted that phænomena in space which, for the most part, demand juxtaposition in order to their being (causally) related, are not to be confounded with even the facts of consciousness, such as volition and its effect. Surely this is a relation of a wholly different nature, either from bodies in space actually placed side by side, and even from bodies which, as in the relation of gravity, act at a distance in space. If the space relation be different even from the volitional relationship, how much more must it differ from the relation of a conscious subject to all the varieties of its known objects? Yet there does not seem to be in the whole of Mr Green's discussion on this point the slightest acknowledgment of the difference—the essential difference in kind—between those relationships. "Relation" is all we hear of it, and it matters not to what it is applied—what it denotes; it is the idea always of relation, and unalterable relation.

But let us see what precisely is Mr Green's doctrine on the subject of relation. Here we must rely on quotations of the author's exact words, for these are not, as a rule, translatable into ordinary language without transparent contradiction. The following are the chief points:—

(1.) The main point in relation is "the unity of the manifold." "Abstract the many relations from the one thing, and there is nothing. They, being many, determine or constitute its definite unity. It is not the case that it first exists in its unity, and then is brought into various relations. Without the relations it would not exist at all."—(P. 31.)

(2.) "The one relation is a unity of the many things. They in their manifold being make the one relation. If these relations really exist, there is a real unity of the manifold,—a real multiplicity of that which is one.

(3.) "But a plurality of things cannot of themselves unite in one relation,—nor can a single thing of itself bring itself into a multitude of relations."

(4.) "The single things are nothing except as determined by relations which are the negation of their singleness, but they do not therefore cease to be single things. Their common being is not something into which their several existences disappeared."

(5.) "If they did not survive in their singleness, there could be no relation between them,—nothing but a blank featureless identity. There must then be something other than the manifold things themselves, which combines them without effacing their severalty."—(P. 31.)

Now, here are two points :—

(1.) The several relations of a thing constitute the unity of the thing—even its existence : without the relations the thing is nothing—would not exist at all.

(2.) But the several relations negate the singleness of the thing, and yet the single thing does not cease to be single. The thing still remains single, otherwise there could be no relations.

These statements are absolutely contradictory, and cannot be held together. If relations constitute the existence of a thing—if, in a word, the being of the thing and the relations of the thing are convertible, and especially if these relations are several—there is an absolute contradiction in holding at the same time as true that the thing is single, or one. Further, we are speaking now only of abstractions called relations, which are impossible alike in thought and fact, apart from a single thing in relation to something else, or single things in a time relation to themselves.

There is a further contradiction in holding that the relations of a thing constitute its unity. The relations of a thing may reveal its unity; they do not make it to be one. A thing could not have several relations—that is, properties—unless it be already one, or be supposed to be one, at the moment of showing the various relations. The self or ego is known to be one in time, because at various successive moments of time it reveals different acts—that is, shows its relations to or in those acts; but our knowing these acts, and the fact of a one self through them, does not make the self one. This only shows us that the self must be supposed to be one, otherwise we could not know it as related successively to different acts. All through there is confusion or assumptive identification of *knowing* and *being*. It is the case that we must suppose that the self first exists in its unity, but it is not the case that we know the self as first existing in its unity. We know that this must be, because we know certain definite relations which it manifests in successive times, and we know that it survives each successive change of state or relation.

The third position is: "A plurality of things cannot of themselves unite in one relation, nor can a single thing of itself bring itself into a multitude of relations."

"A plurality of things" means, I suppose, two things at least. These cannot of themselves unite in one relation. This, I suppose, is because they are a plurality—are, say, two. Two bodies in a given space cannot gravitate towards each other of themselves. They do gravitate towards each other; how do I know it is not of themselves? What put gravity into them, I may not know. But is it not there? And do not the bodies gravitate of themselves, so far as I observe, or can know meanwhile?

The whole is a mere argument from abstractions. "Plurality" must, as a concept, always remain plurality, and "singleness" must always remain "singleness," or unity. But possibly the very things we know are known as related to begin with, and we do not need to abstract either their plurality or their singleness, and contemplate these apart, and then ask ourselves whether the "plurality" or "singleness" can do this or that. Possibly things in relation are what we know, and possibly this knowledge depends on their being already constituted, and what they are.

Further, relation does not necessarily imply "unity" at all. There is relation where there is difference, as in saying a rock is not organised, two is not four, &c. The unity here is secondary; it may be the unity of the person judging, or his relation to the object of thought, but the relation of difference in the matter judged is equally real.

Relation does not imply "the unity of the

manifold." It does not imply that the many is one, but simply that there is one amid or in many. It is one thing to say all things like in successive times are one in respect of the point of likeness, and another to say that the like things are one. The like things are not necessarily one because they are like. If they are like only in one particular, they are not one. If they are like in every particular, they are not one absolutely, because they were experienced or perceived in successive times; and each time constitutes individual difference.

And if the relation be of the one or self to the many of its successive states, there is not any more a "unity of the manifold." The self is one and indivisible amid the states: the sum of the states or of the self in each time in the states—the states+the self—do not make the many states one; they are diverse, individually different, as in different times, nay, it may be of wholly different characters, as feeling, desire, volition.

In the next paragraph, arguing for the need of intelligence to combine the manifold things without effacing their severalty, he holds that it is essential that "one [sensation] should not be fused with the other,—that the distinct being of each should be maintained." He adds, "On the other hand, in the relation to which their distinctness is thus necessary, they are at the same time united" (p. 32). This, he thinks, can be done only by "the action of something which is not either of them or both together." This is "the relating act of an intelligence which does not blend with either" (p. 32).

The distinct being of each is necessary thus to the relation, and yet we have been told that the relation makes, and is, the unity—the being of everything. Is not "the distinct being of each," so far as the relation of likeness or difference between the sensations is concerned, thus supposed as the ground of the relation? How can this be both ground of relation and relation itself?

But further, how can "a relating act of intelligence," which blends with neither, compare and relate distinct things—sensations or anything else —unless it apprehends the things as distinct to begin with, and then finds the point or points of similarity? But if it does this, it must know the things as its own objects; and if objects of knowledge or intelligence thus to begin with, how can it be, as we are told immediately thereafter, "that sensations, as brought into relation by intelligence [*i.e.*, relation to each other], become sensible objects or events"? If sensations are already apprehended as objects to the intelligence, how have they to wait for relations between them to make them intelligible?

But there is a deeper point. Intelligence, it appears, brings these things into relation—sensations, atoms, &c.—everything in the (material) universe, at least. "Relation is the product of our combining intelligence." "Our intelligence is a factor in the real of experience." Is it so? Is it the intelligence which in our world or cosmos constitutes the real for us? the real order? the relations of things? It brings "things into relation," so makes them to be what they are—makes them real for us, in a word. Then have things no relations as given or presented to us, as actually occurring in the course of time, as actually coexisting in space? Are the time relations, the space relations, simply creations of our intelligence? What warrant has this intelligence for its action—its bringing together, combining, relating? Does it do its work blindly without apprehended ground in the things, or does it see relations in things, or what corresponds to relations, and so constitutes our (known) cosmos? There is no answer to this question—no glimpse of it. It will not do to say there is no order which is not an experienced order, and therefore a conscious order. I should admit no such assumption. But even if this were so, I wish to know how intelligence can constitute relations between sensations—relations of various sorts—out of its own spontaneity?

Intelligence is a conscious process,—it is supposed to know what it is doing. When we judge that heat is not cold, or black is not white, or round is not square, why do we make the difference? When we judge that sensations are successive in time, that others are simultaneous, that some are coexistent in space, how does intelligence make the difference? What is its ground or warrant for procedure in each case? Why does it make different relations? On no reasonable ground but on that of a known order, which it does not create, but which informs and illumines it.

We may fairly ask what relations, and how many in any given case, are needed to make the object of experience real? We have before us, for example, the "feeling" we call water. Water has no doubt various relations to other "feelings." As we realise these, water is real. But which of them, and how many? Are they to be what may be called the essential relations or what? Is the "feeling" water not real until it is related to its elements, the "feelings" oxygen and hydrogen? Or is it real when I relate it to its property, the feeling of washing or cleansing? or to its property, the feeling of flowing or fluidity? Or is it real as I think of it as existent,—as now and here,— as in quantity, quality, degree, and so on? If the former be the meaning, and water is not real until I relate it or as I relate it to something else beyond it,—beyond the momentary perception,— then though the present perception gives me an object (of vision), it is not yet real, and I relate what has as yet no reality to something else, and so make it real. I am afraid that if I have no reality in the momentary perception to begin with, I shall never by any process of so relating clothe it in reality at all. And further, if I have to wait for all the actual and possible relations of the percept ere I can clothe it in its full reality, I shall have to wait a long while.

If by relating the immediate or momentary percept be meant referring it to category, existence, quality, degree, &c., or to time and space, I have simply to say that this relation—the particularising of the category—depends on the character of the percept, and is only possible in as far as there is a ground of relation in the object itself, constituted for my apprehension. But if there be this ground, the object is already real,— has its quality, degree, &c., as the condition of my relating it. Its reality does thus not lie in the relation or relating, but in the ground of the relation.

Here is a specimen of reasoning: "Of two objects which form the terms of a relation, one cannot exist as so related without the other, and therefore cannot exist before or after the other. For this reason the objects between which a relation subsists, even a relation of succession, are, just so far as related, not successive"—(p. 34). In other words, two objects which are successive are, so far as related to each other, not successive! But let us hear the explanation:—

"In other words," we are told, "a succession always implies something else than the terms of the succession, and that 'a something else' which can simultaneously present to itself objects as existing not simultaneously but one before the other." What although the succession does imply "something else" than the terms of the succession? How does this make the terms of the succession not successive—not before or after? Nay, there is even a deeper plunge, for the "something else" is actually brought in to present the objects to itself as before and after!

We are not concerned to dispute the position which is so constantly and elaborately asseverated and maintained in this Introduction, that there is a reality in what is the work of the mind,—that all the work of the mind, or what is attributed to mind, is not mere illusion; nor even the position that mind or intelligence is a factor in experience. But it is going much further than this to hold, and to hold as the one necessary alternative, that relation constitutes reality, that relation is necessarily the act of intelligence, our or other, and thus by inference exists only as it is understood, or in an intelligence.

Yet this seems to be the assumption of the whole matter. "Intelligence, or something analogous to it," we are told, is necessary "to account for a relation between material atoms as much as any other" (p. 32). It is hardly necessary to point out that "to account" for a relation may require an act of intelligence; but that it does not follow that the relation, or rather the ground of the relation, can subsist only in an intelligence. Yet this is what is implied; for we are told that "if relations are to be supposed real, otherwise than merely as for us—otherwise than in the cosmos of our experience—we must recognise, as the condition of this reality, the action of some unifying principle analogous to that of our intelligence" (p. 32). Does it follow from this that there can be no relation which is not actually known in or by some intelligence? Or is this identical with saying that "the derivation of knowledge from an experience of unalterably related phænomena is its derivation from objects unalterably related in consciousness"? (p. 34).

Here the question arises—Are there any unalterably related phænomena in outward or physical experience? Are we entitled to say of the laws of nature, that they represent the relations of unalterably related phænomena? We know uniformity between sequences. Are we entitled on any ground whatever to speak of them as unalterably related? Is this not to go beyond actual experience, and to do so without even presenting the semblance of a reason? What is unalterable relation but necessary relation? "I demur," says Jevons, "to the assumption that there is any necessary truth even in such fundamental laws of nature as the indestructibility of matter, the conservation of energy, or the laws of motion."

And what of the phænomena of consciousness? Are these all to be assumed as unalterably related? Is every volition I form unalterably related to me, the willer? Is the word "unalterably" to be applied equally to all physical and to all moral facts? If so, and if all even in the human consciousness be merely "a reproduction of the Eternal Spirit or consciousness," what becomes of moral freedom in any conceivable sense? How can there be freedom, if it is a mere reproduction of processes passing in an Eternal Consciousness which flows partially through me? What is this but veiling in terms of the Eternal Consciousness a universal fatalism, in which each individual partially participates? Call the eternal evolution conscious,—what does that matter to the necessity of it?

Mr Green's position may truly be summed up in one expression—"all is relation; relation alone is." Relation is the real for our intelligence; it is the real for the Divine Intelligence. The terms of relation are not; they have no proper existence for themselves. To this are tacked on various statements to the effect of the distinctness of terms in the relation, and of a relator, human or divine, in the relation; but these have no proper existence for themselves; their being in the relation is their only being. The subject, human or divine, is spoken of as the relator, but his work is always finished for him ere he is, and he is only in the completed work. Relator he is not; related is all that can be claimed for him. Mr Green ignores entirely the ordinary view of relation, rather subverts it, and still tries to keep up distinctions which are only possible on the frank recognition of reality and distinction in the terms of the relationship; and of independence in the relator or conscious subject, human or divine. He ought in consistency to give up the advantages of the ordinary doctrine after discarding its conditions, and let existence flow on as a mere stream of relations, in which human and Divine reality are alike lost, which has its source, if it ever had one, no man knows where, and which goes no man knows whither.—Πάντα ῥεῖ.

The contrast between Mr Green's doctrine and the ordinary doctrine is obvious, but he has not vindicated his own position. As has been well said, " All relations supposes two terms which are not the relation itself; this depends on the former, but the former are independent of it." This is wholly opposed to our author's doctrine. But if he does not admit this, what is the logical result? Why this—that the terms themselves are relations. But if this be so, there is no first or fixed for knowledge, no beginning of knowledge. If every term for us is already a relation, then this relation is already dependent on a prior relation, of which it is impossible for us to have any knowledge. At every point where we attempt to commence in knowledge, the effort is conditioned by an unknown relation, and we may spend our time in the fruitless backward movement of an infinite regress, which, after all our efforts, eludes us as when we began. The truth on this point is:

There is a relation of knowledge between subject and object, but I do not know *how* it is, or how it has arisen. It is the first thing for me, and in order to know at all, I find myself in it or supposing it.

On the other hand, a relation between two things in time, or in time and space, is a relation which I, the knowing subject, apprehend, be it similarity or difference, cause and effect. Two things are in my knowledge, and I apprehend them as related. The things might quite well vary, and so the relation would vary. The relation is thus dependent on the accident of the things being at a given time and place. The relation is thus conditional — hypothetical. But the relation between me knowing and an object known,—the relation of knowledge itself,—is primary, as being the condition under which I know the objective terms and their relation; and though the object in this relation may change, the other term—the subject—does not, but remains permanent, whereas in any objective relation of things each term is variable. The identification of reality and relation is thus belied by the fundamental fact of the relation of the subject to object in all our knowledge. The subject is the one and permanent, amid all objects and all its relations to objects; and in this unity and permanency there is more than any existing relation or the sum of all relations taken together.

What may be called the method, rather the trick—I do not say designed—in all this kind of reasoning, is to take a term or concept already existing, and to analyse it, to show what is implied or supposed to be implied in it; to show that it is related or correlated, and in doing so to treat the term and the different terms which are involved as if they were active, or constituting elements in the general concept. The whole of Mr Green's treatment of relation is an exemplification of this method. There is no consideration whatever as to how the abstract concept or term came to be at all, or to be within our consciousness. It is regarded as a sort of personage, which, when questioned as to its nature and genesis, is seen to deploy into various constituents and relations; and the mere fact of there being such is taken as sufficient to account for its reality as a fact of our consciousness. "Relation," for example, is set or taken up, and then we hear of "unity," and "plurality," and the "manifold,"—what they can do and what they cannot do—and how they are to be got together, by something called "a relator," who is to be "above nature" and "out of time." Is not the first question, Has "relation" a concrete exemplification in our consciousness? On what fact or facts does this abstract term or conception depend? How have we come to have it or to form it? Is it verifiable in experience? In a sound sense, Hume's demand to produce the "impression" to which the "idea" corresponds is applicable in all such cases, to save us either from mere verbalism, or from the assumption that in analysing our abstraction we are dealing with the sphere of reality.

The truth of the matter is, that the concept of Being is wider than the concept of Relation, and is not exhausted by it. It is not exhausted even by the postulate of an eternal sum of relations called a self-distinguishing consciousness. It is wider even than such a conception; the being or ground of those relations to be possibly or partially revealed to man, is itself more than the sum of the relations. And in this we have already transcended the concept of relation. To name the sum of possible relations in the universe, some known and others wholly unknown to us, an eternal self-distinguishing consciousness, is to introduce more than relation into the universe, while relation is declared to be all that is known and all that exists.

It is admitted even by writers like M. Renouvier that *being* expresses something more than this or that relation,—" that it is applied absolutely to all relations and to all terms, to all the phænomena which analysis can distinguish, in so far as they appear, exist, posit themselves, come in any manner into representation." But what seems to be implied in this concession as to the transcendence of being over knowledge at any given stage, is at once cancelled by the statement that " being has an absolute as well as a relative sense, but the first apart from the second is certainly vain, hence all is relative."[1]

The point indicated here is the correlation in our knowledge of such concepts as Relative and Absolute, Finite and Infinite, Perfect and Imperfect, Limited and Unlimited, Time and Eternity, Space and Immensity. It seems to be urged that in each case, the second or correlative concept is vain or empty, seeing that it cannot be conceived or realised in knowledge apart from the first. It is argued that, as dependent on the first in knowledge, it is nothing in existence, or it is identical with the first. All this mode of reasoning seems to me to be a mere quibble, a mere play upon words. It might just as fairly be argued that the first term—the relative, for example—is not the relative but the absolute, and that all is absolute. When I know that there is *this* or *that*, I have definite knowledge. This is the relative.

[1] Cf. Ott, *L'Idéalisme*, p. 105.

The absolute, or what is not yet known as this or that, is the something over and above this actual knowledge, which as yet I do not definitely know. This absolute may be simply what is as yet indeterminate or indefinite to me,—something in itself quite determinate, but as yet not known by me as such, though it may come to be so known. Can it be said at this stage of my knowledge that the absolute so conceived is nothing,—that all is relative in my knowledge,—that this unknown is not as truly, if not as much, an object of my knowledge as the *this* or the *that* which I happen actually to know? Can it be said that being thus absolutely taken, taken out of actual known relation, is vain? Why, then, in this case, we should never know that anything is until we know what it is. But such an absurdity in the face of experimental science!—in the face even of the ordinary principle of causality, which is constantly pointing to the indeterminate as the unknown cause, and acting through this by special ignorance as the spur to all scientific research.

This holds when we take the word absolute for what is out of relation—the point at present in question. But if we pursue the matter further, we may come to see that this is but a starting-point for all the higher questions of philosophy, instead of being, as is implied, their foreclosure.

We are face to face with the indeterminate or absolute at every the most advanced stage of knowledge. There is still always the something beyond the actual relation. Is this to be held for ever as a relation,—a new relation of the same kind we know, only to be added to actual knowledge? Here, then, you get into the all-engulfing bog of the infinite regress of relations: relation in relation — never-ending relation—all is relation. Might we not thus properly say at once, that all but the small speck of science that has somehow emerged is for us chaos?—chaos in respect of origin, cloud in respect of destiny? There are the ever-grinding wheels of relations,—relations that are related to nothing in the past but relations,—to nothing in the future but relations. This is the universe—the world, man, and God. It never had a beginning in an absolute being — in a constitution of relations—seeing there is no absolute; and it will never be gathered up in the absolute, for the same reason. An eternal whirl in the past, an eternal whirl for the future. This is the Universe of Being for us, and absolutely.

Obviously a relation in knowledge necessarily supposes a plurality of terms, and, what is more, it supposes the terms actually related. A term relative to another term—that is, to its correlative

—is not a relative at all, if it be not thought as related to the other or correlative term. A husband is not a husband, he may be a man, unless he is thought as related to the correlative wife. Known relation, therefore, is always dependent on an act of thought or conceiving, and relatives do not exist for us unless as actually related and correlated in thought. What, then, is a relation out of thought? What is *before* and *after*, *here* and *there*, when there is no one to think them together? Does not the relation—the contrast—subsist whether we are there to think it or not,—or any other finite ego? The relation we know at a given time cannot subsist out of our thought; and similarly of any other individual consciousness. But the terms of the relation, as out of the given relation, may subsist, whether we relate them or not—whether we constitute them into relatives or not. And I, or indeed every finite ego, may be ignorant of an infinity of *possible* relations or relatives, some of which, however, we may come to know in the course of experience and science,—may even be ignorant of many of the other relations of the two terms, whose one special relation I happen to know. For the terms are not relatives until I conceive them to be such; they are terms, by me as yet unrelated to other terms. The increase of knowledge means an increase of the knowledge of relations. But the ground-possibility of this lies in the terms themselves,—in their properties, in the sphere of definite ordered existence—in the *cosmos*, which I do not constitute,—which I only partially and with difficulty grasp. Clearly, reasoning from analogy, it may be said that the cosmos, or order of things, is itself a series of related terms, whether I know them or not. Relations known by me, or by any finite ego, are not all relations,—are not the first of all relations. And further, if we are to think of the cosmos as related — with parts, properties, powers mutually connected—we ought to think of it as grounded in thought, as ordered by thought, as sustained by thought, with which ours even is in analogy. But beyond this, definite conception fails us, and the substitution of a sum of relations, or universe of relations, for the actual order and ordering of the world, is to darken, not illumine, our thinking on the subject. It is logically to eviscerate the order of the world, or its meaning as an independent constituted system,—to evaporate every finite ego in the ungrounded abstraction called *relation;* and it is, finally, to resolve God Himself into a sum of relations more nebulous even than the star-dust out of which, some think, the planetary system arose.

A relation, as has been said, is a synthesis; but it is also an antithesis. Even when the relatives really coincide, they are always mentally contrasted. This arises from the fact that relation necessarily implies a plurality of terms. The one—the non-plural, the not-relative, the absolute—is diametrically opposed to the relative. It follows from this that relatives can never be thought as one, or in the unity of a single notion.[1] Discrimination, contrast, is the very life-blood of relativity. Hence, just because things are relative, they differ,—are not one, are not conceivable as one. It matters not whether the relation be one of resemblance or of difference, one of succession or coexistence—one of cause and effect, or of means and end,—there is always a plurality of terms conceived as mentally distinct. And hence no argument can be founded on relation or its so-called unity which would imply an identification of the terms. The just inference is wholly the other way; and simply because we conceive relation at all, we conceive things in relation as different. This is the very *esse* of relation.

This has a very special bearing on the highest relation known to us—viz., that of subject and object, or knower and known. Here, whether the

[1] Hamilton's *Metaphysics*, App., vol. ii. p. 536.

known be regarded as a simple state of the conscious subject, as the quality of a non-ego in time and space, as another self in time,—whether the known be perceived or conceived,—there is always a contrast—a contrast in the very relating. This, in its ultimate form, is the difference of *knowing* and *being known*. It is one thing *to know;* it is another *to be known*. The two are inseparable in thought; they are relative and correlative. Think the one, we must think the other; but think the one *as* the other we cannot. The moment this should take place, the relation itself would disappear. There is no relation in absolute identity,— no relation certainly of knowledge. The relation of knowledge, accordingly, of subject and object, affords no ground whatever for the conclusion that the terms of the relation are identical—identical either in thought or in fact. They are together, and they are contrasted—that is the whole matter.

Finally, in Mr Green's theory the supposition of the eternal self-distinguishing consciousness with its totality of relations, both actual and possible, is evidently intended to afford an explanation at once of the distinctness of the world from man, and of its continued existence, apart from finite consciousness. Now, as it seems to me, this is to go wholly beyond the sphere of relation,—to mistake the whole conception of relation, and its place in knowledge and being.

The world of induction and science is revealed to us—a world in which there is uniformity of sequence or recurrence between facts or terms. We have a law when we can speak of A being uniformly followed by B, or when we can go further and say A is the cause of B, and wherever A occurs it will bring us B. But it ought to be observed that induction is here limited to the relation—to the knowledge of it as necessary in sequence, or the knowledge of it as constant conjunction in coexistence. Induction does not say that the antecedent we have met with in the past will be found in the future. We have had experience of the action of the magnet in the past, but we do not by induction infer that there will be always magnets in the world. All that induction entitles us to infer is, that if we find a magnet again, after our experience of the past, it will show attraction for iron. In other words, what we generalise in induction is a relation,—a certain uniform, in a sense necessary relation, between antecedent and consequent, in this case the magnet and iron. Induction thus, properly speaking, tells us of the subsistence of uniform relations between things, but it does not guarantee to us the permanency of the things themselves,—that is, the causes actually existing in the world. In a word, so far as induction goes, the existence, and even the constitution, of things is purely hypothetical. Given the present facts, given the repetition of the present antecedents, and we may be assured of, may firmly believe in, the present or experienced order among them,— their orderly recurrence, — the permanency of their relations. But this in no wise guarantees to us the continued existence of the things themselves between which this order or definite relationship exists. Relation thus — the whole totality of relations known to science, or even knowable by science—does not explain the permanent or continued existence of a single fact in time or space,—of a single cause or term of knowledge. There is no guarantee of anything except the hypothetical uniformity of sequence, or the constant conjunction of coexistence. And what it is impossible for any one conception of relation to do, is equally impossible for the sum of relations to accomplish. Hypostatise the totality of relations in the world,—actual and possible,—attribute these to a self-consciousness, called eternal or infinite, or anything you choose, —you have still only a sum of relations which, from their nature, are purely hypothetical, suppose terms, do not guarantee the reality of the terms or their continued existence; and thus you have no ground whatever for supposing or inferring the continued existence of the world, whose order, if it exists, is all that is given you in relation. If, therefore, this hypothesis of an eternity of relations existing in a self-distinguishing consciousness be all on which to ground the permanency of the world, and help us to rise above individual egoism or psychological idealism, we have no valid ground whatever for such a position.

V.—TRANSCENDENTAL DEDUCTION AND NATURE.

THE whole of this discussion by Mr Green connects itself very closely with what is known as the transcendental deduction of Kant, and his view that "understanding makes nature." It is not necessary at present to enter into a thorough analysis of the transcendental deduction,—what it postulates as a basis, what it supposes as a method, and other points connected with it. There is, however, one essential point which in the present connection demands notice. It has been objected to the transcendental deduction that it may show all that is in the existence of nature, as we ordinarily understand nature, and of the sciences of nature as we are taught to accept them; but it cannot show either that such a nature exists, or that our accounts of it are accurate.[1]

[1] A. J. Balfour, *Philosophic Doubt*, pp. 90, 91.

The answer made by Professor Watson and others is, "That, as Kant holds 'understanding to make nature' (in the sense of a single objective order of phænomena), to ascertain the forms under which alone an order of nature can be understood is to ascertain laws of nature itself. The question whether such a nature exists becomes unmeaning (such a nature as the only one that can be an object of knowledge or understanding must be). If Kant has answered the question, How is knowledge possible? there can from his point of view be no further question whether such a nature exists as that which is thus known. The functions of understanding through which nature is known are the functions through which, as a nature, it exists."[1] The dualism of nature and intelligence has disappeared.

The transcendental deduction thus professes to be an analysis of the conditions under which it is possible for us to conceive what is called nature. But the nature here referred to turns out to be not what we ordinarily suppose nature to be—something in opposition to intelligence, the one member of a dualism in which intelligence is the other member—for "the understanding makes nature." Now this point must be cleared up. Are we to start with the assumption, con-

[1] Cf. Green, *Works*, vol. iii. p. 151.

trary to ordinary belief, that the conceiving nature is nature, or makes nature? Or that the intelligising nature is nature? If the understanding makes nature, nature is simply a process and product of the understanding. It has, can have, no separate or independent reality. There are not two things—understanding and nature—but one,—viz., understanding and its product, nature. Is this an assumption made as to the meaning of nature to begin with? Or is it the thesis to be proved in the end? If the former, the whole transcendental deduction of the laws or conditions under which it can be conceived or known has nothing whatever to do with the question regarding the possibility of the knowledge of nature in the ordinary sense of the term. And we may throw the whole deduction aside as utterly irrelevant. Here you profess, first of all, to show how, and how alone, I can know nature. This is not what you actually do, or carry out. You, under cover of doing this, show, or seek to show, how something called understanding makes nature—does not merely know it, but actually creates it. This may be true or false in itself, but it implies a shifting of the real issue—a shifting from a process of knowing to a process of making or calling into being. The question which the transcendentalist has here to answer in the first place is,—Is this sense of the term nature to be taken and put in the place of the ordinary dualistic sense? What right have you, the transcendentalist, to assume the negation of dualism? Do you not require a philosophy to prove this? and is this not the proposition which you have got to establish in the end, not to assume at the outset?

This is no answer at all, therefore, to the objection made — that an analysis of the conditions under which we can alone know nature does not imply that nature exists. Let the necessary conditions on which what we call understanding makes nature, or conceives nature, be duly set forth. There is no ground here for saying that there is a nature at all, in the dualistic sense of the term; and all that is really established, supposing the analysis successful, is the conditions under which we are obliged to think how understanding makes or produces something called nature, which is not nature in any real sense of the word. Nay, the setting forth the necessary conditions of a conceivable object called nature is not in any sense the same as setting forth the reality of even that nature, if this be supposed more than simply an object conceived. The conditions of a conceived, understood, or intelligible object are simply the conditions of that object as conceived or intelligible. And if the object has more or other than a conceptual existence, then these conditions will be realised in it, otherwise it would not be the object spoken of. But this is a purely hypothetical statement. It does not carry us forward to the actual reality of the object, or allow us to descend one degree from the lofty region of *a priori* possibility. There is here an ambiguity in the term nature—the confusion of the conceptual reality of an object with its actual or present reality, and an assumption of the identity of the laws of knowing with the laws of being. But the truth is, that no philosophy worthy of the name could pursue such a method as this. It is only a shift to which its advocates are driven to meet objections. The transcendental method, if it is to do anything at all, must start from what is recognised as reality — from an acceptance of ordinary experience, or of some portion of it. It may proceed to say and to show that whatever fact, concept, or principle can be shown to be necessarily implied in that experience or portion of experience selected, must be accepted by those who agree as to the reality of the starting-ground. But this implies a certain common consent to begin with. The transcendentalist and I must agree about the reality of the bit of experience selected. There must, further, be analysis and definition of the experience through ordinary psychological method; and if this is to take in all that is given in experience, or supposed to be given, there must be at least a tolerably complete system of psychology laid down in the first place, and agreed upon; otherwise the basis would be simply in "common-sense" —that dreadful bugbear to the lofty deductionist. And, further, there must be the acceptance of certain logical canons, or principles of reasoning, else we could not tell what is necessarily implied, or only contingently associated in our deduction. Then the transcendental method might be of some use in laying bare the connections and implicates of knowledge; but this practically supposes a prior philosophy, and instead of being, as it is represented, the method of the ground and possibility of all knowledge, it is only an application of principles to facts already ascertained.

The question of the relation of Understanding to Sense, in the perceiving or making of the world of nature, is a vital one for Kant and Kantianism. Does it mean, as Dr Hutcheson Stirling supposes, that there is perception first, and categorising or understanding afterwards? Is there special cognition, and then is it that the understanding through its categories makes the special perception or sense-apprehension necessary and universal? Do we find knowledge in individual instances, and through reflection find that these are embodied in the instances, concepts, and principles which we must think and which all must think?

This view of Kant's doctrine is not admitted by the Neo-Kantians; and we find what is alleged to be the correct account of the doctrine summarily stated by Professor Watson in the following words:—

"When Kant is leading up to his own theory, and simply stating the facts he has to explain, or when he is criticising the dogmatic theory of his predecessors, he naturally speaks as if sense immediately reveals to us special objects or events. From the philosophical point of view, however, sense he conceives of as the faculty which supplies the isolated differences which thought puts together and unites into individual objects or connections of objects. The 'manifold of sense' is, therefore, simply that element in knowledge which supplies the particular differences of known objects; and these differences, of course, vary with the special aspect of the known world, which at the time is sought to be explained."

(1.) "Sense supplies the isolated differences which thought puts together and unites into individual objects or connections of objects."

Nothing in the form of an object is thus presented to thought, or perceived. "Isolated differences" are "supplied" to thought, and thought puts them together,—makes an object or objects of them.

(2.) "The 'manifold of sense' is, therefore, simply that element in knowledge which supplies the particular differences of known objects, and these differences of course vary with the special aspect of the known world which at the time is sought to be explained."

(3.) When, for example, Kant is seeking to show that individuals in space and time are necessarily extensive *quanta*, the special fact of knowledge to be explained is the apprehension of objects as made up of parts forming individual aggregates. These parts Kant regards as directly perceived or contemplated. The "manifold" may be the parts of a line, the parts of any geometrical figure, or even particular figures, regarded as constituents of more complex perceptions; or, again, it may be the parts of individual objects in space.

So far, here, the meaning is perfectly clear, and we have at least an intelligible account of what thought has to work upon in constructing objects of space and time. Perception or sense hands over to it parts—isolated parts or points, say in a line, as not yet, however, made up into a line.

These are perceived as "isolated differences,"— as "a manifold." They are, however, in consciousness — sense-consciousness; and what is called thought gathers them together, — makes one object of them, — in this case, a straight line; and thus individual objects are constituted. Any realistic philosophy may quite well accept this statement. It is an analysis, quite a possible one, of the mode in which space objects at least are conceived by us. Exception, of course, might and would be taken to the assumption apparently made, that when we have accounted for the conceivability of the object,—for the object as in combined apprehension and conception, —we have at the same time explained the genesis of the object as an actual fact or reality. We have explained, in a way, or laid down the universal conditions of its reality as a conceived and conceivable object by us; but prior questions might certainly be raised as to how the perception of each particular point is itself possible. For if we start from this as necessary to the action of the thought which is to constitute the object, we have not explained our knowledge of the object from the beginning; we have but laid down certain conditions under which what is perceived is constituted into what is conceived by us. And there is a further point here: if the particular parts or points—the "manifold," coextensive or successive—be matter of perception, it cannot be true that an object is constituted for the first time by the action of thought which only works upon the perceived data. We cannot deny the name of object to a percept in consciousness: a single percept—a point or part—facing the conscious subject, is as much an object as the more complex object, say line or figure, which is constructed by thought.

But we are immediately told that, though all this be so, " the particulars, as due to sense, are, when taken by themselves, mere abstractions; they are, in fact, not even known *as* particulars apart from the synthetic activity of imagination as guided by the category of quantity. To have a knowledge of the parts of a line, or the parts of a house, as parts, is to know at the same time the combination of those parts. But the combination of those parts takes place for us only through the act by which we successively determine space to particular parts, and in that determination combine them."

Now it seems to me that in this we have the confusion of two wholly distinct propositions, and that from this confusion springs the aberration manifest in the whole of this mode of reasoning. It may be perfectly correct to say that we cannot know the points or particulars of a line,—the parts of a house, of a tree, or object in space, — as the parts of such line, house, tree, without at the same time knowing the whole of which they are the parts. If we say these are the points or particulars which make up this line or that house, we must know at the same time the combination of which we speak as this line, house, or tree. But this proposition is not relevant to infer that we did not know those points or particulars in isolation simply as points or particulars. We may not know these at first as parts of a whole—cannot so know them, indeed, until we combine them; but we may know each as a point or part or particular percept,—each as a present impression in time as opposed to no impression; each as a particular point in space, as opposed to a vague or blank space; and, consequently, we do know them as particulars quite definitely and intelligently. And hence it is a mistake to suppose that there is any negation of the doctrine that particulars are apprehended or known *as* particulars, in the proposition that to know particulars *as* the particulars of a definitely combined whole, say line or tree, we must first, or at the same time, at least, have combined the whole. And yet on this confusion of totally different propositions the whole of this argument is based. It is nothing better than a piece of intellectual jugglery—unconsciously done.

But there is more than this to be said, and it is relevant to the following inference: " Thus, in the knowledge of the line, there are implied both the particular element of sense and the universal element of thought. We do not first perceive the line and *then* apply the category, but *in* perceiving the line we apply the category. And as in all recognition of objects in space we necessarily determine the particulars of sense through the schema, as silently guided by the category, we may express this condition of our knowledge in the proposition, 'All percepts are extensive *quanta.*'"[1] Here the confusion I have spoken of reaches its climax and application. Of course we do not *first* perceive the line and *then* apply the category of quantity, and *in* perceiving the line we apply the category. But this refers to the secondary process, or the result of the combination of particulars already given and known. The moment we get the length of combination, we get the length of quantity—and in perceiving what we have combined, we may be said "to apply" the category,—in a word, to re-

[1] Green, *Works,* vol. iii. p. 156.

cognise quantity, even necessarily. It may even be said that in combining the particulars—in constructing the line—we are doing it under the guidance of the category. But this does not imply that there are no known particulars until, or only as, the combination is effected. It only implies that there are no particulars of that special combination or synthesis.

Nay, more, it would be absolutely impossible for thought, or anything worthy of the name of thought, to act—to construct anything—if it were true that, in the case of a specific combination, there is no percept in consciousness—no particular of sense known—ere the thought has worked and combined, or as the thought is working and combining. There could be no conscious combination of that which as yet did not exist in perception or consciousness,—there could be no reasonable combination. Thought could not take cognisance of the differences in things, could not know what category to apply in any given case, unless the perception furnished the difference to it. The " manifold of sense" is said to supply differences —isolated differences. If these are not by themselves, as opposed to the new character which they assume as parts of the combined whole, known to consciousness—known to thought itself— thought is paralysed, and never could determine the slightest difference in things. It may be—it is necessary—that in knowing objects—sense and thought—the particular and the universal should be combined; but they are not, and could not be combined, in the way spoken of. This supposed mode of constituting objects results either in the impossibility of knowledge or in unreason.

But it may be said that in recognising known particulars prior to particulars in a specific or individual combination, and particulars thus as relative to that combination, you do not escape the application of category to knowledge and the constitution of knowledge through category. The particular impression of a given time, or time and space, implies difference and distinction by the percipient,—implies even the percipient himself, and relation to himself—relation to other impressions in time and space, and so on. All this is true, and essentially true. But in admitting this, nay, inculcating it, there is no divorce implied between perception and thought, as in the interpretation of the Kantian view with which we have been dealing. At the very minimum of perception there is category—inexplicit category, it may be—universal concepts and laws of knowledge—waiting to be evolved in the clear light of reflection. But perception has its place as much as thought. It has to guide thought, as much as thought has to regulate perception. To say that thought "constitutes" the object, or that "understanding makes nature," is unwarrantable, or it is a confusion of reality as perceived with reality as conceived. There can be no more violent or worse abstraction than that which severs the thought of the understood from the perceived, and even arrogates to the former the power of constituting the latter.

"We successively determine space to particular parts." "We" cannot do anything of the sort,— meaning by that the personified abstraction called "thought." "The determination of space to particular parts" is not possible by us, unless as the particular parts are already related to space, and apprehended by us as so related. Every individual thinker might determine as he chose, if there were not a fixed objective—to which his perception and thought are subject. And this opens up the whole question as to the ultimate ground of our knowledge, as well as of the ultimate nature of being.

Therefore, nothing exists out of this relation— in other words, there is no absolute existence,— there is even no existence unless a conscious existence. The whole ground alleged on which the conclusion is based is the inability of the individual self to conceive an object—that is, reality

—in any but such a relation. But am I thus entitled, on the ground of simple inconceivability on my part, to say that related, phænomenal, or known reality is all that is? In the former case, the power or conceivability of the individual was made the ground of the constitution of existence; in the latter case, the limit of conceivability is made the ground of the restriction of being to the sphere of the phænomenal. The known, or knowable under relation, is identified with the whole sphere of reality. In both cases the link of proof is wanting, and the inference equally unwarrantable. Nay, it might be shown that, but for a background of the phænomenal, which is definitely imperceptible, but yet is thinkable and necessarily thought, the phænomenal itself is contradictory—not reality at all. And though this position is laid down as leading to the necessity of a universal self or intelligence which transcends the individual, time, and finite reality, and yet makes them to be, it can be shown to be utterly subversive in the conclusion. If relational or related reality be all reality, a self which is everything—which is absolutely universal in being—is utterly inconsistent with any such conception of the real. It must not be assumed, as is done, that "the thing in itself" is necessarily divorced from the phænomenal—an absolute entity, incapable of receiving a predicate; but as ground of the phænomenal, or known, it does not properly come under the designation of being related to a subject, much less the individual conscious subject, as the phænomenal itself is. It may have to be "conceived" in quite a different way from the time or presented object, and may have a reality not in any way dependent on me or my modes of conceiving, or those of any finite subject whatever.

VI.—EXTERNAL PERCEPTION.

MR GREEN has hitherto worked up to his ultimate conclusion through the two lines of an analysis of Reality and Relation. He now, in the second chapter of the *Prolegomena*, seeks to reach the same conclusion through an analysis of what we know as External Perception. Reality and relation may be regarded somewhat as abstractions; but an analysis of Perception certainly refers to something definite, and we may suppose that if the reality of the Eternal Consciousness can be connected with this, it must have some claim to our belief in the concrete. Let us see.

It seems, according to Mr Green, that popularly, and even philosophically, there exists a confusion "between the perceived object and the exciting cause of sensation" (p. 63). He accordingly proceeds to clear up this point as a fundamental one; for the mistake leads to "an extension of the perceived object from the consciousness in which perception consists, and tò the view of it as an external something to which perception is related as an occurrence to its cause" (p. 64). "The stimulant of the sensation involved in a perception is never the object perceived in a perception." In a perception of colour, for example, the vibration of ether which stimulates the optic nerve is not the object perceived. This may not even be known to exist; it may be only the scientific man who includes this in the knowledge of the perception. But whether known or not to exist, the vibration of ether, as the exciting cause of the sensation of colour, does not enter into the object perceived—into the content of the perception—in the same sense in which it acts as the exciting cause of the sensation. So far, this is perfectly true, and is the commonplace of the psychology of vision. It would have been, however, more accurately expressed if it had been said that the object of perception, in this case the colour, is an object known in quite a different way from that process by which we know—infer—the vibration of ether; that the one is an intuition, and the other an inference of induction; and further, that to mix two such different forms of knowledge in one complex act called perception, is to lead simply to confusion and ambiguity, and to retard the progress of sound analysis. Instead of saying that this inferential knowledge does not enter into the content of the perception, "in the same sense in which it acts as the exciting cause of the sensation," it would have been more correct to say that it in no way enters into the content of the perception, though it may accompany the intuitive act as a gathered knowledge. Hence there cannot be anything but censure for a statement like this: "Strictly speaking, it is not a vibratory ether, but the fact consisting in the relation between this and the optic nerve — this fact as existing for consciousness—that enters into or determines the perceived object, as the scientific man perceives it" (p. 65). In no case whatever, of the scientific man or other, does this "relation" "enter into the perceived object"; it is not known to consciousness in the act of perception; the sensation of colour is complete without it; it is not an object of perception, or part of it; it is a subsequent knowledge acquired by scientific method. All this comes of a loose use of words, based on imperfect psychological analysis. But there is more than this. It is wrong, according to Mr Green, "to suppose that this object or content is external to the percipient consciousness, as the stimulant matter is to the sentient organism" (p. 64). "The sentient organism to which the vibratory ether may be considered external is not consciousness, either as exercised in perception or in any other way" (*ibid.*) The perceived object, however described, is wholly within consciousness; or rather, "the opposition of without and within has no sort of application to it. A *within* implies a *without*, and we are not entitled to say that anything is without or outside consciousness; for externality, being a relation which, like any other relation, exists only in the medium of consciousness, only between certain objects as they are for consciousness, cannot be a relation between consciousness and anything else. An affection of the sentient organism by matter external to it is the condition of our experiencing the sort of consciousness called perception; a relation of externality between objects is often part of that which is perceived; but in no case is there such a relation, any more than a relation of before and after, between the object perceived and the consciousness of it, or between constituents of that consciousness."—(P. 65.)

Now what does this really mean? Is it coherent? Why, is it not rather absolutely contradictory?

Let us take the total object of perception as the scientific man perceives it, without disputing meanwhile about the mixing up of intuition and inference. There is (1) the sensation of colour; (2) the affection of the optic nerve; (3) the cause of this in the undulatory ether; (4) the known relation of this to sensation as effect. The undulatory ether is external to the optic nerve as part of the sentient organism. The ether is not consciousness; the sentient organ is not consciousness; these are external, therefore, to consciousness : yet the moment they become related as external to each other in consciousness—as known to be what they are—they are no longer external to consciousness, for they are thus related as external, and all relation is in consciousness! In other words, things that are external to consciousness,—that exist and act, and yet are not a part of consciousness,—the moment they are known to be external, cease to be external! How can we consistently speak of undulatory ether "external to the sentient organism,"—of "an affection of the sentient organism by matter external to it as the condition of experiencing the sort of consciousness called perception,"—if our whole knowledge in perception be that "of the relation between this [undulation] and the optic nerve,"—if this be wholly within consciousness, and at the same time nothing "which is known or related can be outside consciousness"? Ether, undulation, sentient organism, cannot be intelligibly regarded by us as not consciousness, yet existing and acting, and at the same time as, the moment they are known or related in knowledge, becoming parts of consciousness or within consciousness, and then only existing for us. The two statements are absolutely contradictory; and further, as conditions of perception, they are external to consciousness, but as they are not known in this externality, but only as "within consciousness," the conditions of perception are never known as they are, but only as something else—constituents of consciousness. The conditions of the conscious perception precede all before the perception: these are external; but as known, they are parts—constituents of the conscious perception; these are internal; they are thus both preceding conditions and constituent parts. If there be no *within* and *without* in our consciousness of things as they are, there is neither *within* nor *without* at all—the distinction must transcend knowledge. And to talk of things being *within* consciousness when they cannot be distinguished from those *without*, is a simple break with intelligibility. If "the external stimulant" of sensation, which is the occasion of perception, be known, it must be known in an act of knowledge which transcends consciousness itself, for there is no without and within in consciousness. Nothing is external to it; and perception is in consciousness—is a sort of consciousness. Knowledge, therefore, is wider than consciousness, or we may know and not be conscious of our knowing. This is simply an attempt to ride on the opposite theories of Realism and Idealism at the same time.

It is at this point in Mr Green's theory of Perception that the lack of grasp of the facts as they actually are, and of their bearing on his doctrine, becomes conspicuously apparent. The simple analysis of the process in perception, including especially the organic, is sufficient to expose the whole of the fallacy of the so-called oneness of being with consciousness, or of there being nothing "outside of consciousness." To maintain the oneness or unity of being with consciousness, as it is phrased, in face of even the simple facts of sensation and perception, seems extraordinary. The relation of the ordinary physical or organic conditions to sensation and perception seems never to have been grasped by a certain class of writers. There are certain organic movements which precede or accompany ordinary sensation and perception. These are well known in vision, in hearing, in touch. The extra-organic or purely outward movement in space, undulatory and vibratory, takes place; the terminal organ—

viz., the retinal expanse—is thereupon affected; then the nerve or nerves which communicate with the brain; then the brain centre. We have thereupon the sensation—viz., light or colour. But all those changes of movements, from undulation in space to brain centre, are, as such, wholly unknown to us at the moment of sensation. Of them we really know nothing; they lie wholly beyond the consciousness of the moment. Scientific observation and induction on our part come subsequently, acting probably on organisms not our own, to note and generalise them. It cannot be maintained that these are not outside the consciousness of the sensation—nay, outside the consciousness in succession of every sensation. Will it be maintained that they have no reality, no true existence, because they are outside consciousness — that of myself, that of any individual percipient? Why, they are as real as the sensation itself, though they are not within the consciousness at the moment. They have a definite individual momentary existence, and then pass away—never in their proper individual existence to be recalled. They are a part at the same time of the real world, of that world of experience which I only partially grasp in my consciousness, but which is all the same whether I grasp it or not. I come afterwards to know them, to think of them, to infer them. But will it be maintained that now only at this later stage they come into being, because I conceive them or think them through my consciousness? This supposition is simply ludicrous in itself. Besides, how can I identify the past being of those movements—a being gone never to be again—with my ideal conception of their being long after this first actual being has disappeared? This argument might be extended with reference to all being—all individual being in space and time—which depends for its conceptual realisation either on the image of memory— that is, referring to the past, or on the image of imagination, referring to the future and possible. Oneness with consciousness—the unity of consciousness in this sense—no more exhausts or is convertible with reality than the being of the one moment can be rendered adequate to the being of every moment.[1]

Mr Green then proceeds to develop his theory of Perception. According to him, the constituents of any perceived object "can exist only for consciousness, and the consciousness for which they thus exist cannot be merely a series of phænomena or a succession of states" (p. 65). He adopts, in a way, the account of perception as a synthesis,

[1] On this latter point see Mr Shand in *Mind*, April 1888, p. 231.

and this synthesis is, in his view, one of feelings, but not "of feelings as caused by the action of external irritants on the nervous system, but of known and remembered facts that such feelings have occurred under certain conditions and relations" (p. 66). The former synthesis may be presupposed in perception, but it is the latter which constitutes it. He continues: "No feeling as such, or as merely felt, enters into the perceived object,—not even the present sensation, which is admitted to be a necessary condition of perception. It is not the sensation, but the fact presented by the self-distinguishing subject to itself, that such a sensation is here and now occurring, —occurring under certain relations to other experience,—it is this that is the nucleus on which the recalled experience gathers, suggesting other possibilities of sensation."—(P. 67.)

Let us see how this analysis applies to the facts in any given case. I have a consciousness of *colour* as spread out before me in space, and at a given moment or in a series of moments. This consciousness I may call sensation or perception. The colour, as seen by me, is the sensation. It is felt; but "as merely felt," it does not enter into the perceived object—that is, in plain language, as I suppose, it is felt but it is not perceived. Perception does not arise until I, the self-distinguishing subject, "have presented to myself the fact that such a sensation is here and now occurring,—occurring under certain relations to other experience." If ever there was an impossible distinction attempted, this is one. What is implied in the sensation being felt? What is implied in there being a sensation at all? Why, surely a consciousness of it. Can we name anything a sensation which is not a conscious sensation or conscious state? The affirmative here seems to me not only not to be possible, but to contradict the very meaning of the term sensation, as appropriately used in the history of philosophy. But if a sensation as felt is an object of consciousness or in consciousness, what becomes of this so-called distinction between sensation and perception? What becomes of such a theory of perception at all? If the sensation, in order to be at all, must be in consciousness, then there is a consciousness or apprehension, explicit or implicit, of the sensation as now, or as now and here. The *now* and *here* imply certainly distinction and relation. They imply the specified presence of the sensation in the continuous movement of our experience,—its distinction from, and relation to, other portions of that experience. There is further involved the presence of a self-distinguishing conscious subject, as that through which this sensation and all our other experience is possible. All this the self-distinguishing subject comes fully to know and realise, through certain processes of reflection. It is not by any means a happy form of expression to say that the self-distinguishing consciousness "presents" these facts to itself. It comes to a knowledge of them as facts, no doubt; but if there be any presentation in the matter, there is as much receptivity on the part of the self-distinguishing consciousness as presentation by it to itself. But if all this knowledge be involved in the simple consciousness of the sensation — in the sensation as felt — what does the perception add to it? Perception in this case would merely be a term, and a singularly inappropriate one, for the gradual evolution by reflection of what is involved in the simple act of sensation—say, the sensation of colour or sound. According to the point of view and character of the individual self-distinguishing consciousness, there would be more or fewer of those distinctions and relations apprehended,—the fact of the sensation being or being felt would be the rudimentary one in an objective point of view; its relation to what went before it or to what came after it would be further readily noted; and in a highly reflective person, the self-distinguishing subject would probably stand out in relief. But to call this concentrating and gradually evolving reflection perception is about as bad an application of a word as can well be conceived.

But let us take the other alternative. Let us suppose that the sensation as felt is not in consciousness, and that we have thus to wait until the self-distinguishing consciousness, or subject, presents the fact of the sensation to itself. Now it may be conceded that there are sensations so slight in our ordinary everyday experience that we hardly, if at all, notice them. They come and go, especially in the case of mental absorption, when the mind is otherwise occupied, say, in study or thought, without special regard, and there is little or no memory of them. But these may be thrown out of account, as never amounting to real knowledge—the normal degree of knowledge which constitutes recognition. Attention specially arrested and concentrated on one of those sensations would doubtless render it known and emphatic. Such cases do not come within the scope of the present theory. The sensation in question is supposed to be felt merely; but apparently it is not as yet in consciousness, or we do not consciously distinguish it as an actual fact in our experience,—we do not present it to ourselves as such. But if it be not in consciousness at all, how comes the self-distinguishing subject to deal with it,—to think of it,—to regard it as occurring now and here? How can the self think of it as anything whatever, not to say as *this* and *not that?* The self-distinguishing consciousness must be supposed to be a reasonable being; and such a being certainly would not present to itself as a fact the present occurrence of a sensation which is not in consciousness at all; nor would such a being say that there is knowledge or perception of this sensation as opposed to that —of red, say, as opposed to yellow, or of an odour as opposed to a sound—unless there were in the actual fact of consciousness a known ground of difference. Contradiction, essential contradiction, runs through the whole of this analysis.

I am said to present to myself the sensation, say, of pain or pleasure as a fact, and upon this presentation it only then becomes a fact — in other words, I recognise it as a painful or pleasurable sensation. Is this presentation or recognition of the pain or pleasure as a fact in my experience really the pain or pleasure which I feel? It seems to me to be nothing of the sort, but a wholly secondary or reflex act, dealing with what is already felt, with what is already actually matter of consciousness or experience. That this presentation or recognition is different from the pain or pleasure of the moment is shown by this, that although the pain or pleasure has passed, I can still present it to myself in idea as a pain or pleasure experienced. And, consequently, there is on such a theory no difference whatever between the actual consciousness of the pain or pleasure and the recognition of it even subsequently as a fact of pain or pleasure in my experience. In truth, Hume's idea, or copy of the original pain or pleasure, may be regarded as much a thing of the same kind as the original sensation, if this theory of presentation be held valid.

There seems to be a very serious gap in this doctrine of External Perception, as stated by Mr Green. To put it in intelligible language, we may be said to begin in perception with presenting to ourselves, that is, recognising, being aware of a fact in the way of "feeling," or a feeling as a fact. But this "feeling" seems to be connected by Green with certain organic conditions at first beyond consciousness. In the natural history of the "feeling," the unconscious organic impression is first. But apparently this organic impression, and the feeling following it, of which we take cognisance, or become conscious as occurring in time, or in time and space—depend ultimately, in some way or other, on an Eternal Self-distinguishing consciousness, which is the one side of the multiplicity of relations or things in the world. Clearly, then, the "feeling" is passively determined in us; the "feeling" is the product or result of the action of the Eternal Consciousness. This looks very like Berkeleyanism. As with Berkeley, the percept is ideal, in the sense of being a psychological or psychical fact. We do not find from Mr Green whether he regards "feeling" as a state of the finite consciousness, or as in it, passing through it. The latter is more consonant with the general drift of his doctrine, and if this be his view, it is simply that of Berkeley's "idea." Then we have also the other point that the "feeling" or "idea" or psychical fact is determined in us and for us by the Eternal Consciousness. This may fairly be taken as analogous to the Divine Mind or Spirit of Berkeley. Now if this be so, we are entitled to ask, is this "feeling" or "idea" which our mind is determined to present to itself, the result of the immediate action or inspiration of the supreme self-consciousness working directly on our finite consciousness? Or is it an "idea" or "feeling" which exists in this Divine Mind alone, and which we are permitted to contemplate? If the former, how can it be held that there is "no double consciousness" in the universe; that infinite and finite consciousness are one? If the latter, how can it be said that the finite conscious subject ever had an "idea" or "eeling" determined in it at all? And how can it, being thus virtually one with the Divine, ever be imperfect, or short of the divine knowledge? Then, further, we are left entirely in the dark as to whether these "feelings" are inspired in every successive moment of our consciousness, whether the producing power acts fitfully or constantly, whether the action on every organism is precisely the same; for although we are told of the unalterableness of the eternal consciousness, we, being but imperfectly filled by it, do not know this or anything of it except in so far as it acts upon us. We are just about as far from a solution of the problems of the world at the close as at the outset of such a theory.

There is even the origination of a fresh difficulty. To place the percipient face to face with the action of the divine or eternal; to place it under the immediate causal action of the divine or supreme—the real one cause of all—is to sweep away the whole sphere of secondary or intermediate causes,—to make perception and percept, that is, phænomenon in the outward or real world, the series of psychical phænomena we name such, in all its course and extent, the immediate, even necessary, result of divine power. Whatever sensible anomaly or contradiction,—

whatever sensible experience of pleasure or pain, —whatever sequence of physical evil or suffering —all this comes directly from the divine—is the divine hand at work, if we may speak of the eternal consciousness as an agency at all, and so put into it a predicate which renders it even possible to deal with the course of experience passing on in time. The hypothesis of the eternal consciousness, as held by Mr Green, explains nothing, but adds to the difficulties of the situation.

In fact, it is impossible to classify a scheme of this sort, which says yes or no to precisely the same proposition, which is permeated by contradictions, and remains only as a thin glimmering mist, in which neither the world, man, nor God is recognisable.

Yet the purport of the whole is plain. It is an attempt to minimise—in fact, annihilate—the objective or presented side of Perception to the illegitimate aggrandisement of the subjective side. We are expected, on such a basis as this, to infer that the subject alone, or self-distinguishing consciousness, presents us with the external world out of itself; weaves it, in fact, as a web out of its own consciousness. Psychologically, such a doctrine may only be false, and thus comparatively innocuous; but, ethically and theologically, it has, as we shall see, somewhat serious and vital consequences.

This purpose, indeed, is very soon expressly avowed. We have already been told "that the constituents of a perceived object exist only for consciousness" (p. 65). Now we are taught that "the particular things we perceive—this flower, this apple, this dog—in the only sense in which they are objects to us, or are perceived at all, have their being only for, and result from, the action of a self-distinguishing consciousness" (p. 68).

This is explicit enough. Things "have their being only for," and "result from the action of a self-distinguishing consciousness." We need not at present consider that the self-distinguishing consciousness turns out to be one common to all individuals of the race, and not merely the consciousness of this or that supposably varying individual. It is still a "consciousness" from whose action all particular things in the world result, and they exist only for it. So far as we have hitherto gone, the alleged proof of this conclusion seems rather to point to the impossibility—the negation, in fact—of sense-knowledge or perception at all; a process of knowing which is essentially self-contradictory is of no value as proof of any conclusion. And if what has been said on this point in the criticism already made be correct, there is little need for going further in examination of a conclusion so based. But let us look at it a little specially; and first, of the terms in which it is couched.

(1.) Particular things "in the only sense in which they are objects to us, or are perceived at all, have their being only for a self-distinguishing consciousness." How alone can we assert such a proposition as this? How are we entitled to say that the object in perception, in each and all of the senses, not only taste, smell, sound, and colour, but extension, with all its implicates, and resisting force, exist only as they are the (known) objects of "a self-distinguishing consciousness" or conscious subject; that which distinguishes what it apprehends or knows from itself, and so recognises it? How do we come to think of "a" self-distinguishing subject or consciousness at all? Only through the consciousness each man has of himself as a self-distinguishing subject of knowledge. Until or unless we have this, we cannot speak with meaning of *a* self-distinguishing subject. This is a thing wholly in the air, an utterly unwarranted abstraction, nay, nothing for any one whatever, until or unless as he realises himself as a self-distinguishing power. But what is the result of this?—Why, this; that we are starting from the individual of consciousness; we have analysed what he does, we may suppose, in the act of sensible apprehension, in his relation to the quality merely of a not-self. By what step, I ask, does any one proceed from this individual analysis to the universal assertion here made about "a" self-distinguishing consciousness, or self-conscious subject? Is the analysis of what takes place in my consciousness necessarily identical with what takes place in all consciousness whatever? Is my consciousness and its mode to be set up straightway without further proof as the essential type of all consciousness whatever? Are we to have a self-distinguishing consciousness set up as the universal measure of being, as the type even of all knowledge, merely because I, a self-consciousness, happen to know under certain definable limits? This may be a right or a wrong conclusion; it is one, however, which Mr Green, and others who follow him, have not attempted to prove—have, in fact, illegitimately identified with a simple supposed analysis of the individual self-consciousness.

The vicious method of philosophising represented by Mr Green and his followers cannot be more emphasised than just at this point. The analysis, or supposed analysis, of what takes place in my individual consciousness is forthwith, and without the slightest attempt at adducing a reason, attributed to a distinguishing self-consciousness—that is, to all or every self-consciousness; and further, this abstraction so illegitimately clothed is set up as the type of all self-consciousness, and the condition, even the measure, of all existence. The whole question is precisely the value and import of individual experience or consciousness, and the man who ignores this misses the primary question of philosophy.

It comes, then, to this, that at the least we cannot attribute to the action of a self-distinguishing consciousness more than fairly follows from the action of that self-distinguishing consciousness which we know, and which, in the first instance, at least, we call *ourselves* or *self*. Now the question arises: Are we entitled, on the ground of the action of our self-distinguishing consciousness, to say that perceived objects have their being only for, and result from, the action of a self-distinguishing consciousness?

I am conscious of a resisting force, which I distinguish quite from myself, in the sphere of space in which I make an effort to move. This force is opposed to me in every way, to my will, to my muscular effort, to all my power. It is beyond me in space,—in opposition to my personality. It is as distinctly something not belonging to me as anything that can be conceived. I experience its resistance, its existence, at a particular time and place. Does this force exist only for my consciousness, and is it the result of my self-distinguishing consciousness? Suppose my fruitless effort withdrawn, does the force which opposed me cease to be? Does it cease to be again capable of opposing me the moment I renew my effort? If not, how can it be said to exist only for my consciousness, or to be the result of my self-distinguishing consciousness? Is there not here a gross and palpable confusion of perceiving and being, that is, of knowing and being, while not a word of proof of the identity of these is adduced?

Supposing, in a word, that we do perceive an object only as we are a self-distinguishing consciousness, does it follow necessarily that the object has no possible existence apart from its existence as perceived by us? We distinguish ourselves from the object or percept. Does this at all imply anything about the reality of the object beyond this, that in the act of knowledge the thing is distinct from ourselves?—is a not-self? Are we entitled on this ground to say that its whole reality is identical with its perceived reality? That it may not subsist apart from the time of our perception, either as it is or in some form capable again of appearing to us as an object, even an object similar to what we now perceive? Nay, is not rather the self-distinguishing a suggestion of the possibilities of existence out of the moment of actual perception? And if we are not entitled absolutely to identify *perceiving* and *being* in the case of our own self-distinguishing consciousness, how are we warranted in doing it in the case of *a* or *any* or *every* self-distinguishing consciousness? Here the inference, and it is a crucial point, wholly breaks down.

The position taken up by another distinguished writer[1] on this point seems to me to be substantially the same as that of Mr Green, though the latter does not admit the identity. He even criticises it as a subjective method, or an appeal to "thought as a subjective process," and holds that "an unwarrantable inference is drawn from the power of conceiving to the reality of that which is conceived."[2] He seeks to correct or supplement it by the statement of what may be taken as his own method in these words: "To assume, because all reality requires thought to conceive it, that therefore thought is the condi-

[1] Principal Caird, in *Introduction to Philosophy of Religion*.
[2] *Works*, vol. iii. pp. 143, 144.

tion of its existence, is unwarrantable. But it is another matter if, when we come to examine the constituents of that which we account real—the determinations of things—we find that they all imply some synthetic action which we only know as exercised by our own spirit."[1] And this is, that all things have their being in relations. I think Mr Green's objections to the "subjective process" thoroughly sound; but I fail to see that they do not in substance apply to his own method, which professes to look at the determinations of things, and to infer "a thinking consciousness" to account for the union of the relations, because "we know no other medium." What is this but to found on the power of conceiving? As the method to which Mr Green refers is, as seems to me, unsound, and the source of erroneous inference, it comes in here for relevant notice. The passage quoted for comment by Mr Green is certainly a typical one, embodying as it does the main argument of the book. Part of it is as follows :—

"To constitute the existence of the outward world, or of the lowest term of reality we ascribe to it—say in 'atoms,' or 'molecules,' or 'centres of force'—you must think them or conceive them as existing for thought; you must needs presup-

[1] *Works*, vol. iii. p. 145.

pose a consciousness for which, and in which, all objective existence is. To go beyond or attempt to conceive of an existence which is prior to or outside of thought, 'a thing in itself,' of which thought is only the mirror, is self-contradictory, inasmuch as that thing in itself is only conceivable by, and exists only for, thought. We must think it before we can ascribe to it even an existence outside of thought."[1]

We have here the statement that we cannot conceive an object—say, atom—without supposing a consciousness or conscious subject for whose thought or for whom it exists. This is apparently identified with the statement that the object—atom or element—does not or cannot exist before or outside of a consciousness or conscious subject; that it can only exist for thought, or if conceived. To this it may be said, it is true that I or we cannot conceive an object without implying that I conceive the object, and without implying that the object exists as an object of conception. An object, if conceived, is an object of conception, or for thought. But is this the same as saying that if an object—say atom—be not conceived, it can have no existence whatever? or does the latter proposition follow from the former? Is this first statement the same as saying that

[1] *Philosophy of Religion*, p. 156. See also p. 236.

the object conceived has no other kind of existence, never had any other kind of existence, than that it now has—viz., a thought or conceived existence? Does it necessarily rise into being with my knowledge of it? and if not, what warrant have I for saying that it cannot be unless as in some consciousness? The existence here spoken of is the existence of the object as conceived. It is a wholly subjective reality, and obviously I cannot have a thought or conception of an object which does not exist in my thought or conception. This is true of me and of every thinker. But is this the same as saying, or does it in any way follow from this, that the object of my conception only so exists, or has no other existence than in this subjective relation to me or some thinker? Because the object conceived or thought necessarily exists as an object conceived or thought, am I entitled to say that "there is no existence which is prior to or outside of thought"? When we think or conceive on object—say atom or molecule—we no doubt in a sense may be said "to constitute the existence of the object," but we do not necessarily constitute "the only existence" of the object. To state the latter proposition on the ground of the former is simply a piece of as yet unwarrantable dogmatism. Even in external perception, where we have apprehension and conception of an object—say force in resistance to our locomotive effort—the object is "constituted" for us as an object of knowledge by our apprehension of it; but are we entitled straightway to say that the whole or sole reality of the object lies in its being apprehended by us, or in its conceived and certainly passing reality? When we say an object "is only conceivable by thought," is this the same as saying an object "exists only for thought"? To me it seems there is an obvious confusion of two distinct propositions; and if the latter is supposed to be an inference from the former, it is an illegitimate inference.

But, further, the argument is self-contradictory. An atom or molecule cannot exist before thought, that is, before a self-conscious subject which conceives it, or apart from such a subject, because it is only conceivable by thought. At the same time, we are told that the reality of the world does not depend on our conceiving it; this reality subsists whether we perceive it or not, existed before we were born, and will exist when we are no more. It follows, therefore, that the reality we perceive or conceive, as the world, has an existence outside of our thought or consciousness. Its existence, at least, does not consist in its being related to us. And we are told we can conceive this. "The world, and all that is therein, we can conceive to be as real, though we, and myriads such as we, no longer existed to perceive and know it."[1] How, in the face of this, can it be maintained that we cannot conceive being or reality outside of consciousness? We can conceive being or reality at least outside of our consciousness—nay, of every individual consciousness like ourselves. Where, then, is the guarantee of the alleged inability on our part to conceive reality outside of consciousness in general? If we can so conceive it in our own individual consciousness, what becomes of the ground of proof that a consciousness is necessary to its existence in the universe? The whole ground of this proposition is abandoned, our inability to conceive in a particular way given up, and the general or universal assertion of the need for a conceiving consciousness to constitute reality remains only gratuitously made.

The way, accordingly, in which the supposed contradiction is here reached, is by setting as contradictories two propositions, the one of which is not the negative of the other. The one proposition is, No object is conceivable unless by a conceiver or thinker; the other is, No thing exists unless as the object of conception by a

[1] *Philosophy of Religion*, p. 157.

conceiver or thinker. But the former proposition does not imply the latter, either immediately or mediately, and the latter proposition does not negate the former, and therefore cannot be set up as its contradictory. I say, not immediately, for the terms are not identical, and they require to be proved to be so. Not mediately, or by proof, for the ground of proof would be that no object, unless as conceived by some thinker or a consciousness, exists. But that is the very proposition in dispute, and the whole reasoning is a mere *petitio principii*.

I may notice here in passing what, without disrespect, may be called the "stick argument," first introduced, if I mistake not, by Professor Ferrier. It is one of the two main fallacies which vitiate his *Metaphysics of Knowing and Being*. It has been frequently repeated, as obviously triumphant. It amounts to this : You cannot conceive one end of a stick without conceiving the other,— you cannot conceive the circumference of a circle without conceiving the centre,—you cannot conceive an object without a subject. You can distinguish these from each other, but you cannot actually isolate them. Therefore, you cannot conceive the one end, the circumference, the object as existing without the other end, the centre, the subject. Therefore, further, the latter

—end, circumference, object — does not exist without the former. It is curious to find that any one who reflects upon or analyses terms should find any cogency of proof in such an argument as this. All of these are in truth simply identical or tautological propositions—mere hypotheses of definition or abstraction; and the drawing out of what is implied in the subject of each in the form of an explicit predicate adds nothing whatever to our knowledge, far less guarantees any real connection in existence. We simply do not contradict ourselves, or say anything inconsistent with the subject of the proposition,—say only what is implied in what we lay down or conceive.

The so-called argument is really this: Every object implies a subject, because it would not be an object as defined and abstracted by us without a subject; as every effect implies a cause, because it would not be an effect as defined and abstracted by us without a cause. Every end of a stick implies another end, because it would not be that which we call a stick without two ends. This is simply a piece of weak tautological verbalism. The true question in reference to object lies back in the concrete, and is as to whether every thing known to us has but a known reality or a reality during the moment of cognition. The negative of this question is confessedly assumed as the conclusion of the piece of tautological verbalism. What would Hume have said to the argument, that because every effect implies a cause, every change implies a cause?

The truth is, that the formula "subject and object" is an abstraction; it represents what is common to all acts of knowing—to perception, memory, imagination, conception alike,—but it tells me nothing of the question as to the distinctness or continuity of the thing known, in the moment of cognition, and after it has passed. It says nothing of the nature of the object; whether the thing known by me is distinct from me as a reality, whether this may be object to another knower, whether it may subsist and be again to me the object I knew before. The abstract formula—object implies subject—says nothing of the nature of the thing I call object, nothing of the variety of the objects of knowledge. It may be percept—that is, quality of a non-ego, image as in memory, concept as in thought, state of consciousness as in feeling,— all this is left out, slurred over, in the abstract formula, subject and object, and falls to be decided on the grounds of the concrete fact, not on that of the arbitrarily abstracted formula,—of what may be common, while no account is taken of difference. In fact, it amounts practically to this—I cannot know without knowing something. What that something is, whether it is distinct from me, whether it is continuous in being with the moment of knowing, what are its relations to existence, even to other minds, this formula—that if there be (known) object there must be a (knowing) subject—leaves wholly out of account.

Further, it may be noted that to talk of "thought" as the *prius* of things, because in order to know a thing we need to think it, is really a most inaccurate form of speech. No thought can be said to be prior to its object—these are contemporaneous. Even if taken as an abstraction, they are still in one and the same indivisible act at once. And the thought has no more right to be taken as prior than the object of it. The act of thinking—the thought and its object—are together, be it in time or in thought. And because an object conceived supposes a thought or act of thought, this implies no more the priority of the thought than the priority of the object, without which the thought cannot be. If we are to talk of priority at all in this case, it should not be of the thought which is an act, and never existent without an object, but of the thinker and his power, which admits of stimulation by the object, of that which passes into the definite form of the object. This view about thought being the *prius* of things is evidently supposed to be Hegelian. It is really not so. Hegel would not properly look upon thought as the *prius* of things; he regarded thought—in this case, category—as the thing, and the evolution of categories as the evolution of the universe.

We are told that there cannot be an object outside of consciousness, because we must think it before we can ascribe to it an existence outside of consciousness. Why, this statement is belied in every step taken by science, almost in every step taken by ordinary inquiry. Every cause we do not know of a given effect, every substance in which a phænomenon may inhere, is as yet an existence outside of consciousness. A cause we suppose; the particular cause we do not know. How, then, is the existence of the special cause negated by our ignorance of it, or dependent on our knowledge of it? Will it be maintained that there is nothing more or other in the particular cause than there is in the category of causality, and that the knowledge of the latter is identical with the knowledge of the features of each individual cause? This would only be another proof of the absolute divorce of the Hegelian conception of things from fact and experience, and the utter uselessness of it in the real course of life.

But is our conception, with its limits, to be taken as the test absolutely of all reality and all possibility of the real? May what is actually conceived, what is definite, not be transcended at any given time? We can try to conceive cause upon cause, all back through time: we know what this means, but we know that we can never accomplish an actual conception of cause upon cause in endless regress. The conception is impossible in thought so long as we are subject to time conditions. But simply because we have no actual or realised conception of an infinite regress, is this necessarily an impossibility? It is so in point of fact, if we are to set up the actually conceived or conceivable as the standard of reality.

Then we have another allegation of a similar character, as the basis of the philosophy inculcated. It is given in these words, "All that I think, all objective existence, is relative to thought in this sense, that no object can be conceived as existing except in relation to a thinking subject."[1] What of this, we may ask? On whose thought is this conceivability laid? What is "in relation to a thinking subject"? Would such a premiss in any case warrant the inference that nothing exists unless in relation to a think-

[1] *Philosophy of Religion*, p. 157.

ing subject? This is apparently the conclusion. I or we cannot conceive an object unless as so related to myself, or to some other conscious subject. The same proof of the same conclusion has been attempted in other words. In fact, it is the stock-in-trade argument of all modern idealists, whether of the individualistic or absolute type. Thus it is said by another writer of a different school: "We affirm that there is an existence out of consciousness which we can only know in so far as it is in consciousness. In other words, we affirm an independent existence, whilst by this affirmation we give it the lie." This amounts to the assumption that if we know, what we know only exists in or as a part of the conscious act of knowing, or it becomes consciousness. An existence cannot be separate from knowing, if it be once known. There is nothing in experience—nothing in any law of intelligence to justify this assumption. An existence may be "in the consciousness," in the sense of being known by us, and yet have a proper independent existence apart from our knowing. It does not necessarily become a part of our consciousness, or our consciousness in any form. It does not necessarily sink to the level of the passing existence of the conscious act —all experience belies this. It is while we know it and as we know it; it may be while we do not know it, either exactly as we know it, or in a potential form capable of again appearing in knowledge. To say that a thing "is in consciousness" is merely to say that we know it; and to dogmatise as to its non-existence when we do not know it, is to put a meaning amounting to a *petitio principii* into the phrase "in consciousness." In fact, the statement, instead of proving a contradiction, is the very suicide of knowledge itself.

But it may be said, as it is otherwise put, that the expression, an unrelated object, is meaningless for us, and cannot, therefore, be or exist; that into which we cannot put meaning cannot be. If we take this proposition in its universality, it would simply consign to the limbo of the non-existent everything not yet discovered by science, and into which as yet we cannot put a meaning. If we take it in a restricted form as to the essential condition of the constitution of any object of knowledge whatever by us, it will imply (1) that the unrelated has no meaning, while the related has—an assumption which is obviously untrue. We know the meaning of the unrelated, as well as we know that of the related. Or it will imply (2) that above the relation or relating of objects nothing has a meaning, which is also untrue, seeing that the relator has a meaning, and that even in certain absolute systems the relator is far from being known in his totality. Or it will imply (3) that because, as we can conceive an object only as in relation to us, relation by some intelligent is necessary to the existence of any object, which has been shown to be groundless. Or it will imply (4) that that which has absolutely no meaning for us can be spoken of as non-existent; whereas such a (so-called) subject of thought admits of no predicate whatever, whether existence or non-existence, beyond being that which is not expressible in a term or synthesis of terms. And this is at the root of the whole bad reasoning. We do not and cannot put a definite meaning into things until they become objects to our consciousness, and until they exist as objects of conscious thought. Up to that point we may deal with terms, but not objects or subjects of predication. But we are not entitled on this ground—the negative condition of our knowledge—to say anything about the existence or non-existence of things, of the actuality or possibility of the world, to transform the condition of our knowledge into the condition not only of all knowledge, but of all being.

But there is even a more serious flaw in all this mode of reasoning. There is the confusion of two wholly different sides of knowledge under the vague term *thought*. There is thought in conception; there is thought in perception or intuition. Thought as conception of an object, of which alone in this connection we hear, is ideal or notional. The existence of the object conceived is for this form of thought wholly notional; it is a mode of reality wholly different from that which appears in thought regulating perception. We may quite well admit that the ideal reality of the object of the concept is constituted by the conscious subject working under certain conditions. This applies to category, and to generalisations from experience. But the reality of the percept, even as regulated by thought and its laws, is a very different thing, and cannot, in any intelligent view of the matter, be said to be constituted by thought or by the thinking subject, in the same sense in which the object of a concept, be it generalised or universal, is constituted. What a writer has to do is not to assume the identity of those two kinds of knowledge, and to reason on this assumption. He has got to analyse them, and to show that they agree, so far at least as his purpose is concerned. And that has not been done. The ambiguity of the word "thought," its constant unanalysed employment in recent philosophy, has become a positive weariness and copious fount of evil.

"Thought" properly means the abstract concept, as opposed to "thing," or it may be to "feeling," "desire," "will." This abstraction has no meaning unless as a concept realised by some thinking subject—either I or thou—or some intelligence of analogous constitution. Yet it is constantly used as if it were a person—the conscious subject himself—and usually credited with what is called synthetic power. Nay, it is used even assumptively, as if it were the only reality, or all reality. As a concrete expression, "thought" may mean either the thinking subject, or the act of that subject in any given case, or the product of the act realised in the consciousness of the subject. It is used for conception, or the grasp of the general or universal in knowledge. It is used even for perception or intuition, which is limited to definite conditions of time and space. These are opposite, some of them conflicting, senses; yet in a certain style of philosophical writing the term is employed as if it had but one, and that a strictly definite, meaning. Advantage is taken of this vague connotation, unconsciously probably, as the meaning may suit the case in hand, and so disastrously for the interests of accurate discussion and progress in speculation.

But let us note in passing how, on this form of

the absolutist theory, we get to the universal self, and what this getting means.

"In thinking myself, my own individual consciousness and an outward world of objects, I, at the same time, tacitly think or presuppose a higher, wider, more comprehensive thought or consciousness, which embraces and is the unity of both. The real presupposition of all knowledge, or the thought which is the *prius* of all things, is not the individual's consciousness of himself as individual, but a thought or self-consciousness which is beyond all individual selves, which is the unity of all individual selves and their objects, of all thinkers and all objects of thought."[1]

Now let us suppose that I, the individual thinker, am conceiving or apprehending something not-me in my experience; that I am confronted, as I truly am, with a *non-ego*, or quality not in the least mine or belonging to me—what is the link of proof in the further proposition that I at the same time know a self-consciousness which is beyond my individual self and all individual selves,—which is even the unity of all individual selves and their objects—of all thinkers and all objects of thought—of me and not-me? I confess the link is to me wholly a blank. I do not find a single item of proof of such a new proposi-

[1] *Philosophy of Religion*, p. 158.

tion. I can make my individual self, like other things, an object of my thought. True,—but in so doing, am I not still simply my individual self of the present time dealing with my individual self, either as past or present? What is really the ground for saying that I, the individual self of this moment, standing confronted with something not-me, do in that knowledge know a universal self in which I and the not-me are fused in one? If this be so,—if in this sense I transcend myself,—what becomes of me and my knowledge? Can I any longer be said to know when the difference between me, the self, and the not-self is abolished, and the two are fused in one? Nay, how can I be said to distinguish the two sides, or know anything of the two sides at all, if every time I know, or think I know, I necessarily recognise that I and the object not-me are really one, and I am fused in a universal intelligence or self which is both? Can I keep my individuality and laws of knowledge under difference and plurality while I am merged in one universal self which is both me and what I know? Nay, can the words knowledge, truth, fact, reality, on this supposition, have the slightest meaning?

When I know or apprehend myself and something not myself in the same indivisible act of cognition, I am said to transcend myself, and necessarily to know or apprehend a universal self-consciousness or intelligence, in which I and what I know or apprehend are one. Even if I am obliged to transcend myself and the not-me as a condition of my knowing, am I obliged straightway to think a universal self, and to regard it as a real self in the sense in which I know myself to be real? This is the crucial point of the whole theory as thus put, but a more complete *saltus in concludendo* could not be given. If I grasp myself and a not-self in one and the same act of cognition, I no doubt have a two-sided conception. But how has my individuality, therefore, disappeared in a universal self, which is both me and the not-self? The one statement, instead of being implicative of the other, is directly contradictory of it. To try to save the opposition by saying that you can distinguish, while you cannot divide or separate as independent, the one from the other, is merely to cloak the absurdity in a form of verbalism. You cannot distinguish the one from the other. You cannot have an individual self, much less a series of individual selves, and at the same time one universal self; you cannot have at the same time subject and object, or self and not-self, in any sense, and one universal self which unites all selves, and both subject and object.

It may be said—it seems to be assumed—that the existence of a distinguishing self-consciousness is needed for the subsistence of the object perceived—for example, force in space. Now I do not say that the mode of the subsistence of force that passes out of my perception is easily explicable, or explicable at all. Here, possibly, we may be face to face with the mystery—the insoluble mystery—of being. But I may have evidence from experience—inferential proof—that the force or object does exist in some way or other, in a sphere transcending my perception. This, in fact, is the lesson of science in its simplest form. It teaches the reality of the insensible constituents of the world in the form of atom, ether, corpuscle, along with and involved in the sensible. These are not and never can become objects of perception, that is, phænomena in the proper sense of the term. But the point at present is, Does the supposition of the reality and subsistence of *a* self-distinguishing consciousness—not necessarily *me*—to whom this force continues to be a perceived object, serve in any way to render the subsistence of the force out of and above my individual perception explicable or reasonable? On this hypothesis, the object perceived—the force—is handed over, as it were, to a self-distinguishing consciousness, who takes care of it until I need it again for my perception. One would like to know the ground or grounds, in the first place, for the assertion of such an ego; one would like to know further whether this other ego is a counterpart of my ego or self-distinguishing consciousness— an older or a younger brother. If he is, I fear he will have the same difficulty as I have in keeping a continuous hold of the perceived object, and therefore in his turn will need to hand it over to a third ego of similar constitution and capacity, whose powers will be similarly tested, strained, and baffled, so that, in order to keep up the subsisting being of the object, it will be necessary to go on, *ad infinitum*, conjuring up egos or distinguishing self-consciousnesses, and so the chance of the recovery of the object thus handed about will be infinitesimally small. And certainly the force, after passing through all those mystic forms of air, would have but little prospect of being again recognised by me.

Or if we put this supposition in the form of one universal self-distinguishing consciousness, or ego, framed in our conception after the model of our own individual ego, but stripped of certain limitations, indeed all limitations, set above time, and yet capable of keeping in its perception or consciousness the time-objects of perception, and so holding them in continuous being—we shall get probably the theory after which the writer is toiling. This hypothesis will be examined in the sequel on its own merits. At present all that need be said is that, even if it were admitted, it can afford no reasonable or conceivable ground of explanation of the subsistence of that which I perceive in time and space, seeing that this ego, so-called, has not the slightest relation to either.

But let us look at perception on its objective side. We have constant talk here of the object, the object perceived, the real nature of the object, and so on. We have to ask, (1) Can we, on this theory, have an object in perception at all? (2) What is the real nature of the object as perceived, according to this doctrine? Let us take Mr Green's own words:—

"The real nature [of a flower] consists in relations of which consciousness is the medium or sustainer. It is not, however, with the real nature of the flower, but with its nature as perceived—a fragment of the real nature—that we are here concerned; and it is relations of which the percipient consciousness is the sustainer, which exist only through its action, that make the object, as in each case the percipient perceives it, what it is to him."—(P. 68.)

We have here as constituents of the real nature

of a sensible object (1) conscious relations, or relations of which consciousness is the medium or sustainer; (2) which exist only through its action; (3) which make the object what it is to the percipient. Where is there any objective residuum or ground whatever? Where is there anything but conscious relations or relations in consciousness? What is the so-called object perceived but the perceiving itself—no longer apprehensive of aught out of itself, but a simple process of relating,—in a word, a perceiving without a percept—a relating without terms to be related? This impossible action of consciousness is called the object perceived—the real nature of the thing, as perceived. The truth is, there is no longer any object; there is simply perception without a percept, and relation without a ground. Pure abstractions—in fact, mere words—are treated as realities, and the whole real world of experience vanishes under the process. This is the arbitrary, unverified and unverifiable process of the whole of this order of philosophising. It violates every rule of good sense and of accurate philosophical method.

But a point for the theory here emerges, which receives very scanty consideration. It is somewhat lightly stated in the following words :—

"Facts related to those of which the percipient

is aware in the object, but not yet known to him, can only be held to belong to the perceived object potentially, or in some anticipatory sense, in so far as upon a certain development of intelligence, in a direction which it does not rest with the will of the individual to follow or no, they will become incorporated with it. But they become so incorporated with it only through the same continued action of a combining self-consciousness upon data of sensation through which this object, as the percipient already perceives it, has come to be there for him."—(Pp. 68, 69.)

This introduces us to the question of the future of perception or knowledge—of its growth and development in experience—under conditions of time. Clearly the relations, or, in other words, the properties of any given object of perception which future research may develop, are numerous, indefinite, we may say illimitable. This is especially true if we take the object not only in itself as a percept, but in its possible combinations with other objects. Properties, relations of the perceived object, will emerge of which we did not dream at first, and these will become incorporated with our conception of the object.

And, what is more, our knowledge will not only develop in respect of the possible attributes of the objects in relation to new objects with which it may be in the future connected, but in respect of the actual constitution of the perceived object itself—or what, therefore, has taken place in the past, ere the object became a percept for us. Thus the percept *water* will appear to us in the simplest perception as possessing certain properties or relations—such as *surface, clearness, fluidity;* but we may come also to know, and so to incorporate with our conception of it, its constituents, *oxygen* and *hydrogen,* of which the mere perception gave us no idea.

Now on the theory before us we are told that such facts—all the facts not known to the percipient at a given time—are to be held as belonging to the perceived object "only potentially or in some anticipatory sense." And by-and-by a or the self-distinguishing consciousness at work will in its usual fashion incorporate them with the actually perceived object. Now, no doubt, what a thing can do, but has not yet done, may in a good sense be said to belong to it "potentially." It is a power of action or development existing in it, — as motion is in the pent-up water—as the stem and leaf are in the seed—as the fruit is in the blossom. But looking even to this, the future development of the percept, is it satisfactory to say that the action or property as undeveloped belongs to the actual percept or object perceived only potentially or in an anticipatory sense, so that growing knowledge or increasing consciousness adds it to the object? Is not the property, the power, there now in the percept, whether I, the self-distinguishing consciousness, as yet know it or not? Is it correct, is it even rational, to maintain that the new property as it comes into my knowledge also comes into being? Yet what other interpretation can be put on the statement that these new properties or relations "become incorporated with the object only through the same continued action of a combining self-consciousness upon data of sensation, as at first made the object said to be perceived"? What is this but to say that growing knowledge is increasing creation? What is "a combining self-consciousness" here but the self-consciousness of the individual—or of each individual, working in time? for everything is necessarily known from the beginning to the universal self-consciousness, whatever that may mean. This cannot be supposed ignorant of future properties or relations. The self-consciousness which adds to or incorporates with the object new properties is a time-consciousness struggling with ignorance, and yet, as it is growing in knowledge, means things growing in being.

But what of the other properties or relations of the object perceived, of which we are ignorant during our perception, and which yet make up the object itself? What of the undiscovered elements—viz., oxygen and hydrogen—which make up water? What of the whole field of chemical analysis which reveals the constituent elements of leaf and stem? These become incorporated with the object perceived, as in a future time we come to know them. But, unfortunately for the theory, these were in the object perceived from the first, and made it, unknown to us; and but for these, it would not have been even the limited perceived object it appeared to us. And yet it is a or the self-distinguishing consciousness working in time, and through ignorance, which is making them and adding them to the object—incorporating them with it! This is an emphatic instance of the conclusions which result, and must result, from the unwarranted confusion of knowing and being in metaphysics.

In fact, if we were to take this part of the theory by itself, we should at once land not only in creation by the self-distinguishing consciousness working in time, and so gradually casting off its ignorance, but we should have a purely arbitrary or fictional creation, each individual ego working precisely as it pleases. Clearly, if it be the self-distinguishing consciousness which makes the perceived,—if there be nothing thus which, lying out of its range in a fixed manner, determines the relations which it perceives or constitutes—its action may be, for aught we know, wholly arbitrary. There is neither standard nor check for its action. We might have as many worlds as there are individual egos to make them. But Mr Green will not have this; and it is thus necessary for him to find some fixed objective standard or power of control higher than the individual ego,—who is ignorant to begin with, and yet creative as he goes on, but who is kept in order by, shall we say, a higher self-distinguishing consciousness than himself, or one with which somehow, in the end, he comes to be identified. Here is the first indication of the superintending and controlling power: "Objects do not cease to be 'objective'—facts do not cease to be unalterable—because we find that a consciousness which we cannot alter or escape from, beyond which we cannot place ourselves, *for* which many things indeed are external to each other, but *to* which nothing can be external, is the medium through which they exist for us" (p. 69).

This passage contains what we may call rather a subtle conveyance into the discussion of a new point. It is not argued that the arbitrary nature of the action of the individual ego would not follow from the conditions of its action just laid down, but we, the individual egos, are at once confronted with "a consciousness which we cannot alter or escape from, beyond which we cannot place ourselves," "as the medium through which things exist for us." Hence, therefore, our action cannot be arbitrary; we are bound hand and foot to this—"a consciousness"—and out of it we cannot for a moment get. We had heard repeatedly before of "a" self-distinguishing consciousness working on the data of sensation, and making this into fact or object perceived, and quite superior to mere succession in time,—and we were not warned that this meant anything but each individual ego endowed, it may be, with a common function, and coming somehow in different places and times to tolerably similar results. But now "we," while still appearing or not extinguished, are confronted at once with "a consciousness" which holds us as tight as if we were the prisoners of fate, and will not allow us the least latitude of fiction in the making of the world. This easy offhand introduction of "a consciousness," to which we are somehow related, is the vital point in the theory, in as far as it moves towards its conclusion. And a great many questions of the utmost importance at once confront us. We may ask—Is there this consciousness? On what grounds is it alleged to be? What precisely is it? How is it revealed to us, or to the "we" for whom it is the unalterable medium of knowledge and being?

VII.—THE ETERNAL CONSCIOUSNESS.

THE main ground of proof of the Eternal Self-distinguishing Consciousness, is founded on the analysis of Sense-perception already given. Perception, it is alleged, as established, requires, in order to the presentation of the simplest component of the whole perceived, "the action of a principle of consciousness, not itself subject to conditions of time, upon successive appearances,—such action as may hold the appearances together without fusion in an apprehended fact" (p. 70). Again—"The ordinary perception of sensible things or matters of fact involves the determination of a sensible process, which is in time, by an agency that is not in time" (p. 71).

It seems to me, on the other hand, that such a principle has not been shown to be necessary to ordinary perception, or to any perception. What may be taken to have been proved is quite a different proposition. It is that in the apprehension of an object in relation to another object before it, or to other objects of which it is one in a series, there is needed, over and above the objects or terms of the succession, a continuous subsisting principle or subject conscious of each momentary object, and capable of holding all of them before it in one conception as the parts of one series in time. It is true that this conscious subject is not in the series, in the sense of being one of the terms succeeding; it transcends in a sense each of the terms, it transcends even the series; but "above time" or "not in time," or "not itself subject to conditions of time," it is not. It is a one principle or knowing subject which subsists through the moving terms of the series; which by a conscious act knows each term as it succeeds and passes, in the time of the term; which is, therefore, essentially and necessarily in time at each point in the succession; which is further necessarily in time, when the given or definite succession terminates, and when it represents to itself the various successive presentations that make up the whole which it *now* knows and did *not* know *before*. The fallacy here lies in confounding the conscious representation at the close of the series which is in itself one and indivisible—the concept of one definite succession, with the knowledge which progresses to the completed synthesis; and because this in itself is not a succession of terms, holding that the subject conscious of it or which makes it is "not in time." It further lies in identifying the superiority or transcendence of the subject to the terms or times of the known succession, with its superiority to or aloofness from "the conditions of time." So far from a subject of this nature being necessary to perception, perception would be impossible if the percipient were subjected to any such conditions. Yet it is mainly on such a ground as this that we are asked to take the step, or rather make the leap, to the existence in the universe, and as the ground of the whole facts or relations of being, of an Eternal Self-consciousness, variously described, and, as we shall see, dubiously and confusedly related to that of the individual-ego.

We ought also to note at this point the exceedingly inaccurate statement of the accepted realistic view on this matter. It seems that, according to this doctrine, no synthesis of sensations into objects is required to be performed by the conscious subject: "objects are supposed to be there independently of any action of our minds; we have but passively to let their appearances follow each other over the mental mirror. The succession of such appearances, and of the mental reactions upon them—reactions gradually modified through accumulated effects of the appearances—may fairly be taken to constitute our spiritual being" (p. 69). This is simply a rough statement of a sensational view of consciousness, which every sound realist repudiates. This is not, as is assumed, the only alternative to Mr Green's view; and it is a specimen of the intellectual unfairness which characterises him, and most of his followers and writers in the same line. They are constantly presenting an extreme alternative of this sort as the only one. It is not so in this case, as any one ordinarily familiar with the representative writers on the realistic side knows. The alternative to a conscious subject above time, yet doing work in time, is not a merely successive consciousness, or rather set of conscious impressions, got from an independent order of external phænomena; but the very different and not irrational conception of a conscious or spiritual subject, continuous in time, exercising a synthesis on an order of facts, for purposes of knowledge, yet rendering the conception of succession possible. And this doctrine does not confuse the conception of the singular indivisible unity of the subject,—one in the midst of the passing terms,—with its superiority to the conditions of time.

But the process of proving from the self-consciousness in perception, which is above time, goes on. It might be that this was a theory of sense-perception and no more. But it is to have a much wider extension than this. It is to be applied not only to the perception of fact, but to the facts themselves. Facts, or relations of objects in our consciousness, do not come into being when a man attains knowledge of them, or cease to be when his knowledge ceases or he forgets. There is a universe of facts, or of relations, quite independent, it would appear, of the individual consciousnesses of the world, which have a time-history. The perceiving consciousness "seems to vary from moment to moment; it apprehends processes of becoming in a manner which implies that past stages of the becoming are present to it as known facts; yet is it not itself coming to be what it has not been?" (p. 72.) Have we not, then, here got to an antithesis? And is it that the relations which the perceiving consciousness constitutes are not the real relations of the universe after all? Or are the universe-relations identical with those made by the perceiving ego working on sensation, acknowledged to be in time, and event in time? We shall see.

The universe-fact, if we may so speak — the objective, unalterable fact, — implies, nay is, a relation. "Fact always implies relation determined by other relations in a universe of facts; and such relations, though they be relations of facts to each other in time, imply something out of time, for which all the terms of the relations are equally present, as the principle of the synthesis which unites them in a single universe" (p. 71). Facts being relations, necessarily exist only for a consciousness or in a consciousness. The analogy of the perceiving consciousness is transferred to the universe, or universe-consciousness; and as perceived reality is simply relation in time by a subject out of time, so is all the reality of the universe, or rather the true and only reality of things. Fact — reality — then, means ultimately relations of events to each other in time, subsisting in a consciousness or principle out of time, which unites them in a single universe. There is a (or one) consciousness, or self-distinguishing subject, for which the relations or facts that form the object of our gradually attained knowledge already and eternally exist; and the growing knowledge of the individual is a progress towards this consciousness (p. 75). This is "the eternally complete consciousness" (p. 72).

Here, then, we have the further question as to

the precise relation of this eternally complete consciousness to " our consciousness "—the consciousness of me as an individual, and of every individual in the world. The answer is thus given:—

"'Our consciousness' may mean either a function of the animal organism which is being made gradually a vehicle of the Eternal Consciousness, or that Eternal Consciousness itself, as making the animal organism its vehicle, and subject to certain limitations in so doing, but retaining its essential characteristic as independent of time, as the determinant of becoming, which has not and does not itself become. The consciousness which varies from moment to moment, which is in succession, and of which each successive state depends on a series of 'external and internal' events, is consciousness in the former sense. It consists in what may properly be called phænomena; in successive modifications of the animal organism, which would not, it is true, be what they are if they were not media for the realisation of an Eternal Consciousness, but which are not this consciousness."—(Pp. 72, 73.)

This is a somewhat remarkable statement as coming from an idealist, and shows, what the whole course of absolute idealism discloses, that it is identical ultimately with absolute materialism. We might have naturally and logically expected that the Eternal Consciousness, holding the relations which alone are real, would have directly communicated with that self-consciousness which we know and are. In our self-consciousness — even in its lowest form of our perceiving consciousness — we yet are not conscious of dependence on a bodily organism. If there be an eternal self-distinguishing consciousness — far above time and space — we might have expected the spiritual to communicate with us directly, on our spiritual side — the universal soul touching directly the time-soul, — spiritual, too, in its essence and power. But no; this is not the new and advanced conception. "Our consciousness" — that part of the eternally complete consciousness in which we are permitted to participate — is "a function of the animal organism"! Do we but communicate with the Eternal Spirit through the animal organism? But let us for the moment take it so. "A function of the animal organism" — yet is there nothing external to consciousness? — to the Eternal Consciousness? The Eternal Consciousness is struggling, striving, even baffled with "the animal organism" called man! — trying to interpenetrate it. Yet all is in the Eternal Consciousness. A relation, therefore, this animal organism in the Eternal Consciousness, — a relation which it makes — which is only as it is in it,—yet which baffles its development! A more illegitimate dualism never was called to the needs of absolute idealism. A consciousness "varying from moment to moment," "consisting in phænomena," "in successive modifications of the animal organism,"—this is the human consciousness, or our consciousness. It is not consciousness at all, in any proper sense of the term, but the identification of consciousness with a material non-ego, illegitimately and contradictorily borrowed by the idealist, with a view to depreciate the true consciousness which psychology reveals. This too is done in the interest of an abstraction called the Eternal Consciousness, which, by its timelessness alone, is absolutely divorced from the whole world of experience.

But we are immediately assured that there is, after all, "not a double consciousness in man;" only "the one indivisible reality of our consciousness cannot be comprehended in a single conception" (p. 73). I should think it could not, on this system at least. It would be exceedingly hard to fuse in one conception a consciousness described as a series of varying, successive phænomena, modifications of the animal organism, with a one consciousness described as eternal—that is, at once for ever what it is, not subject to conditions of time, and yet really the same with the successive consciousness, the function of the animal organism. There can be no conciliation, no such fusion. There can be no indivisibility of reality in such a conception, for the simple reason that there cannot be framed by the mind an object corresponding to such conditions. The human consciousness we know has disappeared, and in its room we have an abstraction, not only unverified and unverifiable, but null through hopeless contradiction.

But we have admissions as to "processes organic to our consciousness," "events affecting the animal system organic to consciousness" (pp. 79, 82, and elsewhere). These, it seems, are "determined by the mind to which all things are relative"—that is, the Eternal Consciousness; and then this consciousness reproduces itself in our knowledge or consciousness, "in respect at least of its attributes of self-origination and unification of the manifold" (p. 82). The whole bodily organism, accordingly, in as far as it ministers to knowledge in sense or perception, is the thought or thought-relation of the Eternal Mind or consciousness. It is not the sign of the thought of this mind—something different from that which it expresses; but it is actually the thought or thought-relation of this Infinite Consciousness. Brain, sensuous organ, nerves—afferent and efferent—spinal chord, &c., are all simply thought-relations in the Supreme Mind, or at least the one mind of the universe. But in perception we do not perceive or know these. They are the conditions of our sense-knowledge; but we can have, actually have, ample sense-knowledge, without being conscious of them or knowing anything about them. At the same time, this sense-knowledge is, after all, the act — the thought-relation of the one consciousness — which awakes in us to sense-knowledge. As in us, therefore, this consciousness may be, nay, is, actually ignorant at a given moment of perception—of thought-relations which exist only in itself. And if these relations exist at that moment, they must be in the thought of this consciousness, which is at one and the same time ignorant of them and conscious of them. That is the pass to which we come. The one consciousness of the world is like the moon, to this extent, that it has a dark side and a light side. Only as the light (or conscious) side by hypothesis alone exists, the dark (or unconscious) side, while necessary to the light side, has, as dark, no existence. Or if the thought-relations summed up in the organism are known to the Eternal Consciousness *per se*, though not known to it in man, or as connected with this organism, it must know in one of its functions or sides that of which it is ignorant in the other. It is a compound of knowledge and ignorance regarding the same thing. What now becomes of the "one consciousness" of which we hear so frequently? If a house so divided against itself can stand, most contrarieties will.

I am in no way concerned to dispute the position taken up by Mr Green, to the effect that man, as a consciousness or better conscious being, is not a part of nature, in so far as nature means organism, organic function, and so on—in plain words, a body and nerve system. It may even be admitted that this system is "organic to consciousness" or knowledge in man—though, I think, in speaking thus the writer is undesignedly playing into the hands of the materialist. The latter would make short work of Mr Green's eternal mind or consciousness working on the organic part supposed to condition our consciousness.

Even supposing these objections did not hold, the description of the relation between the eternal consciousness and the time consciousness is enough to condemn the theory. In the animal organism called man, the Eternal Consciousness (or universe consciousness) is constantly making relations, related facts—that is, reality. It is making them in time, and it is "reproducing itself" in these time relations. It is in itself complete; the universe is complete in it, "in its timeless unity of knowledge." There is no succession in the Eternal Consciousness, but one omnipresent now. In what sense can this timeless spirit be said to reproduce itself under conditions of time and succession, or facts related in time? How does the timeless one become the timed manifold? Is it enough to say that the universe, regarded as independent of the individual consciousness, is a series of relations for a consciousness? That all independent relations are necessarily conscious relations? Be it so: how does this enable us to see or to say that one supreme consciousness, not in time, for which these relations exist, does or can reproduce itself—that is, its conscious relations—in those of an individual consciousness, admittedly developed successively or in time? The fact and its relations are in our knowledge determined as now, in relation to past, present, and future. How is this a reproduction of the timeless? And what guarantee have we that our time determinations are identical with the timeless determinations of the Eternal Consciousness? How do we know that the former even correspond to the latter? What guarantee, then, have we of the truth of our determinations? Either the timeless and the time consciousness are different, and then we have no warrant for asserting the relations which each knows to be the same; or the time consciousness is the same consciousness as the eternal, only with a different name or in a different aspect: then, in that case, it is distinctly improper to say it reproduces itself in man. It is the Eternal Consciousness alone, and there is no reproduction in the matter. After all, there is not thus an eternal and an individual consciousness, but one consciousness flowing through all consciousnesses, having, however, lost its timeless character, and being identified with the sum of finite consciousnesses. We get substantially the same result from the consideration of the Eternal Consciousness and the relations of which it is the subject. It is the unity of the manifold; and "the determining and determined," we are told, "cannot be really separated." The one is necessary to the many; the many to the one. The Eternal Consciousness is not without its relations; and the relations are not without the Eternal Consciousness. They are relative and correlative. There never was a time when the Eternal Consciousness determined those relations, for then it would have existed without them; there never was a time when the relations existed to be taken up into the Eternal Consciousness, for then there would have been a universe as yet unrelated to consciousness. Neither was first—both sides are equal in this respect. Each is necessary to the other; the Eternal Consciousness depends for its meaning—that is, its being—on the relations; the relations, for their meaning or being, on the Eternal Consciousness. But the relations are, after all, what we call objects and the laws of objects, which we come gradually to know. The relations are the universe—the objective universe of the senses and of science. Until these relations are thus displayed and realised, they are wrapt up in the timeless inscrutable unity of the Eternal Consciousness. This consciousness then, after all, is dependent for its meaning — that is, its being — on the world of time and space; nay, it *is* this world of objects and relations, unwarrantably named an eternal consciousness. As the consciousness of man expands, so, and only so, does the Eternal Consciousness: nay more, it not only grows in width of knowledge, but it thus grows in being, —truly realises itself, grows out of its timeless severed unity in increasing human knowledge of relations. And thus, instead of saying that the human consciousness is dependent on the eternal, and that it is merely a reproduction of the latter, it would be more correct to say that the eternal consciousness depends for its reality on the human, and is a simple reproduction in the form of a hypostatised abstraction of the human consciousness itself.

As to the extremely critical point of the relation of the universal self to the individuals of time, we are told by one who may be regarded as a follower of Mr Green that we must have recourse to "hypothesis."[1] Yet this is a philosophy which scorns humbler systems, and professes to lay bare the universe! It is actually reduced to "hypothesis" at the point where the origin of the highest reality known to us in experience—our own conscious selves—comes to be considered. There is here a complete gap in knowledge: the gulf yawns between the two sides unbridged, and yet this occurs in a system of absolute unity in knowledge and being!

We are told on the point of the relation of nature and mind, that, "as a process in time, nature precedes mind, and mind is the outcome of nature, yet nature only exists as an intelligible system *for* mind."[2] This is utterly irreconcilable with other parts of the theory. Nature, apart from us, exists only in the Eternal Consciousness above time. In this there can be no before or after; nature is as essential to mind in the eternal self as the latter is to it. There never was pre-

---

[1] *Mind*, No. L. p. 258.   [2] *Ibid*, p. 259.

cedence, and to talk of mind as the outcome of nature is to contradict the vital point of the whole theory.

That thought-relations make the world—are in fact the world — this is the essential point of the theory, and consequently if we had "a complete knowledge of everything in the whole infinity of its relations, this would mean the making of the thing. . . . If I knew another individual person through and through, I should *be* that person. Just because we do not fully *know* our own selves, we never fully *are* our own selves."[1] This is actually advanced as a serious metaphysical argument. We are obviously in imminent danger of losing our individuality, owing to too great intimacy with our neighbour! But what, it may be asked, becomes of the unknowing neighbour in such a case? Does he, too, lose his individuality, and become me? And what is the compound which results from this complete fusion? This loss of the self in another self through knowledge which necessarily constitutes that self, may be a perfectly logical deduction from the system: if so, it is a simple *reductio ad absurdum*.

But, after all, the Eternal Consciousness turns out to be somewhat of a failure in regard to

[1] *Mind*, No. L., p. 261.

knowledge, or rather realising its own knowledge and being. It is terribly hampered by limitations, owing to its vehicle the human organism, and to its having to make progress in time. Apparently, if it had been content to stay "in its timeless unity," it would have been complete; but, for some unexplained reason, it has to go out of this into time, whether voluntarily or compulsorily is not clear, and there it practically breaks down. "The reproduction," we are told, "has a process in time for its organ; therefore it is at once progressive and incapable of completion." The Eternal Consciousness can thus never realise itself in man, " because of the constant succession of phænomena in the sentient life, which the Eternal Consciousness, acting on that life, has perpetually to gather anew into the timeless unity of knowledge" (p. 77). There is a conception that there is a whole order of things, but we can never fully know it, or the Eternal Consciousness cannot know it in us (p. 77). In other words, if the Eternal Consciousness keeps its hand closed in the timeless unity of the manifold, it is perfect, complete; if it opens its hand and so expands to the manifold, it is at once baffled and imperfect. Time and the facts of time are too much for it. It fails to grasp them completely. "The constant succession of phænomena in the sentient life" apparently baffles the Eternal Consciousness, and frustrates its complete development in man. But we have been repeatedly told that the Eternal Consciousness makes all phænomena and their successions. There is no order of phænomena in the universe independent of the relations which subsist in the Eternal Consciousness. Otherwise there would be an order of things external to the Eternal Consciousness—a supposition, above all, not for a moment to be tolerated. The Eternal Consciousness, accordingly, in the only form we know it or can share in it, is baffled by its own phænomena—its own relations; creates what it cannot master, spins ropes which entangle it, or is constantly employed in weaving a web which it never completes. It is perpetually working up material "into the timeless unity of knowledge," whence it is supposed to have emerged; but it can never overtake the whole contents of time. Time is long, but art is short. The eternal power of knowing and being thus remains in the end baffled and discredited. The Reason comprehending itself is a phrase for Hegel's system; the Reason baffled in comprehending itself would apply to Green's Eternal Consciousness. It is never able to complete for itself the knowledge of the world as a whole in man. It gives him, however, the general conception that there is a whole to be known; and so far as the Eternal Consciousness can go, man has the satisfaction of knowing this, and the conviction that this consciousness in him is impotent to achieve the ideal which it sets before him. For the pitcher he brings to the eternal fountain is either too small, or it has no bottom. We thus come back very much to the teachings of a less pretentious philosophy, according to which

> "All experience is an arch where through
> Gleams that untravell'd world whose margin fades,
> For ever and for ever when I move."

But in this philosophy we have not lost hold of the facts of life, nor sacrificed the reality we know for shadows and hurtful abstractions.

We have seen that consciousness—consciousness in general, especially the Eternal Consciousness—suffers nothing to be external to it. This, of course, would be arrant dualism. Consciousness is "that *for* which many things are external, but *to* which nothing can be external" (p. 69). Things—feelings—in (our) consciousness may be related as successive. There is thus a time externality — a before and after. But in the Eternal Consciousness, while there is relation there is no succession. It is a timeless whole, comprehending all actual and possible relations. Our consciousness is admittedly short of the whole. It fails to realise the fulness of the Eternal Consciousness, or rather, this consciousness fails to realise its own fulness in us. It is therefore not in our knowledge; it is not a relation determined or determinable by us. In its own being it escapes,—transcends us. Is there no externality here, different from the mere externality of successive states or feelings, of successive relations? To say nothing of the absurdity of supposing the timeless unity divided,—part in our knowledge and part not,—is there not an essential externality between the timeless unity and our limited and time consciousness? What stronger externality does any dualism demand than that I, a consciousness in time, should be hopelessly and for ever severed from the Eternal Consciousness in its completeness above time? And yet this system is put forward as absolute idealism, and the solution through unity of the order of the world.

Further, as to the development of the Eternal Ego, there is a serious difficulty. Looking to the fact of the degrees of knowledge, education, culture in individuals,—these must be admitted to be of the most various and unequal sorts. There is the state of the savage, the child, the man of ordinary knowledge, the man of science, the poet, the philosopher. History and actual experience show the greatest possible diversity in attainments,—in degrees of development. Yet all in each is the manifestation of the Eternal Ego. What, then, determines the variety and limitations which we know to exist? Is the impediment to an equal development in all due to anything in the Eternal Ego itself, or is it due to outside influences and obstacles,—say, difference in the animal organism, and in outward circumstances generally? If the impediment lie in the Ego itself, what are we to think of its absoluteness, completeness, and omnipotence? Is it not thus as eternal and infinite, holding within itself a baffling element, a simple contradiction? If the obstacle lie in the organism or in outward circumstance, what becomes of its unity,—of the monistic theory implied in it? Have we not thus a dualism, and a confronting, thwarting, irreconcilable Non-Ego? a Non-Ego in the shape of the lowest form of materialism, — merely animal organism. An Infinite Ego which develops in all, but is never perfectly developed in any, from causes which it cannot control, falls simply into disintegration among the animal organisms of time.

Why thus set up such a hypostasis as an Eternal Consciousness, which, complete in itself, utterly fails when it touches practical life?—

which cannot then, though omnipotent, and really all that is, give effect to itself. Why set up a hypothesis which, on touch with the facts of life, is an absolute failure? Why not leave us rather to the working out of the lessons of life through the openings of experience, as these come for us in the course of time, and in the development of intelligence, apart from an Eternal Consciousness which necessarily swallows up all our personality, and leaves us but the "vehicles" of fate, touched with consciousness?

And with his self-distinguishing consciousness, be it eternal or in time, can the philosopher draw from it one single fact—one single relation—that matter of which it is so full, and through which it subsists?—Not one. He cannot from his point of view give you the most elementary fact or law in God's universe. He has got to wait for them through the method of observation, and then, forsooth, in a lofty and lordly manner, to determine each—to make it. But what provision is there for the making of these in simply a self-distinguishing consciousness,—call it Eternal or in time? If there be but a self-distinguishing in consciousness, how can this do anything but distinguish from itself? And how can this simple self-distinguishing give anything but a simple non-ego? How can it give the variety in things, in objects and laws, which we know is to be found in this universe of ours? It is, of course, utterly helpless. If even one thing differs from another in our experience, idealism is discredited—fails utterly. It knows nothing, can know nothing, of an outward which it has not created. How can it reasonably discriminate in this outward, with nothing but its self-distinguishing function? with nothing fixed or determined in the outward? with nothing presented to it? On the scheme of absolute idealism, variety in the objects of knowledge is impossible. And with the failure alone to account for this, idealism perishes.

But it may be asked, What precisely is the ground of inference which is supposed to connect our experience with this Eternal Self-consciousness? Supposing it admitted that our self-distinguishing consciousness does unite the manifold of our experience into objects of knowledge—that it has the unifying power or function spoken of—does it follow at once that the uniting power at work in constituting the reality of nature is necessarily a self-distinguishing consciousness exactly of the same character as our own? and, secondly, is such a power sufficient by itself to explain the objectivity? How are we entitled to say that the unifying power in nature is a conscious power, because we, a unifying power in knowledge, are a conscious power? The power at work in nature may be above nature—non-natural—not one of the phænomena unified. But does it follow that this power must be a self-distinguishing conscious subject, because I, a self-distinguishing conscious subject, unify phænomena in my knowledge or experience? Supposing there is independently of me a uniform objective order which I call nature,—and this, it should be observed, is not proved even to exist on Mr Green's system,—am I shut up to attribute this uniformity directly to a self-distinguishing consciousness like my own? Is it not conceivable that the power immediately at work in this system is a force not conscious of itself, or of its work, or of its ends? This may not be the whole or the ultimate power in things. This power may even be a controlled and regulated power, but if it is even a possibility, this is sufficient to disprove the necessity of a self-distinguishing consciousness like mine as the sole ground of a uniform system of nature. It is quite possible that the unifying power which I know as myself in my experience is but one of the unifying powers at work in the universe. Analogy of function does not imply identity of agent; similarity in effect does not imply identity in cause. Is there really anything more inconceivable in this intermediate force being at the command of an Eternal Spirit, than there is in supposing that the bodily organism is "the vehicle" of the Eternal Consciousness? If this be possible, or conceivable even, far less asserted as true, how can it be said that a force in the universe, subject to the action and control of the Eternal Spirit, is inconceivable, inadmissible, far less unreal? Is not this supposition of an organism, through which the Eternal Consciousness seeks to move, and which it seeks to animate, simply on a par with a force objective to itself, which it constitutes and controls?

Then, further, is such a self-distinguishing consciousness sufficient to create and to sustain the order of nature? Is there really, after all, an identity even in function? I, a self-consciousness, combine and co-ordinate for the purpose of knowing. Is this conscious combination sufficient for the purpose of being, which is independent of at least my knowledge? Is the ongoing of nature precisely similar to the ongoing of my consciousness? Is the objective reality here supposed precisely identical with the succession of feelings, percepts, &c., in my consciousness? Is the mere sustaining of these in and by a self-distinguishing consciousness, called eternal, an adequate ground for their actual reality, permanency, and uniformity? No attempt is made to show that

R

this is so. In a word, it is simply assumed that objective independent uniformity in reality is necessarily the same with the process essential to my knowledge of sensations and percepts—these being nothing more to me than forms of succession in my consciousness. As we know, so the world is; as the object known depends for its being known on a self-distinguishing consciousness, so the world, as existing, depends for its reality and permanency on a self-distinguishing consciousness. A more complete hiatus in reasoning could not be adduced.

But the theory leads further than this. We must suppose, if it be true, that the uniformity of nature—the actual existing relations among things —never had a beginning,—are eternal, unchangeable, unalterable as the eternal timeless consciousness on which they depend, and which constitutes them. In other words, the relations of the order of nature which come partially into our knowledge, which are discovered by science, and which are realised in our experience, in this planet of ours, and what we know of other things adjoining in space,—are the only possible relations, laws, truths of nature, in the universe of being. Are we, on any ground of fact or reason, entitled to say this order never had a beginning in time, that it is the only order of things, fixed, unalterable, and consequently that it can never have an end? What is this but rash assumption and unwarranted dogmatism? What is it but to confound two wholly different orders of truths—the contingent generalisations of experience, and the unchanging laws which lie at the root of our intelligence? It does not even provide for the distinction between laws of fact or phænomena, and the whole sphere of historical truths on the one hand, and the necessary consecutions of mathematics on the other. The necessary unchanging formulæ which the astronomer applies to phænomena are not distinguished as to the character of unalterableness from the shifting phænomena themselves. The star which may be extinguished to-morrow is as unalterable a fact as the geometrical law which expresses its relations to the rest of the system.

A curious light is cast on the theory when the author proceeds to connect it with our actual experience, and especially with what he is pleased to call freedom, or man as a free intelligence. Here he has at once to face the notion and the fact of causality. He is clear enough as to the nature of what we call cause or causality. It is "the relation of a given event, either to another event invariably antecedent to it, and upon which it is invariably sequent, or to an assemblage of conditions which together constitute the event, into which it may be analysed" (p. 80). Such a cause, he adds, is not a "free" cause. Those antecedents are in their turn invariably determined by other antecedents, and the sum of conditions depends on a larger complex (p. 80).

The term cause, therefore, as thus commonly understood, and as realised in our experience, is not applicable to the Eternal Consciousness, or one mind which unifies the universe, and makes even the relation of causality itself possible and knowable. The antecedent is in the first place different from the consequent—the sum of conditions from the effect. But the one Eternal Consciousness is not different from its manifold of thought-relations. It distinguishes itself from the manifold—it unifies it—" but it must not be supposed that the manifold has a nature of its own apart from the unifying principle, or this principle another nature of its own apart from what it does in relation to the manifold world. Apart from the unifying principle, the manifold world would be nothing at all, and in its self-distinction from that world the unifying principle takes its character from it; or, rather, it is in distinguishing itself from the world that it gives itself its character, which therefore, but for the world, it would not have" (p. 80). This is the conception, if it can be called, of the relation of the Eternal Consciousness and the world of being. "The agent must act absolutely from itself in the action through which that world is,—not, as does everything within the world, under determination by something else. The world has no character but that given it by this action; the agent has no character but that which it gives itself in this action" (p. 81). It is added, "This is what we mean by calling the agent a ' free cause '" (*ibid.*)

Clearly, the notion or category of cause can have no application to this agent or principle of unifying, which has no nature or reality apart from the unifying, and is only the unifying. There is no plurality of terms here, as in the causal relation—no antecedent and consequent. This so-called agent is not, unless as unifying or relating a manifold; and the manifold is not, unless as being unified or related by the agent. But why in this case retain the terms agent or principle at all? What right have we to apply words which imply a nature in the agent, a plurality in the relation, and an efficiency in action—when not one of these things is admitted to exist? Why also speak of mutual action in such a case, where there is not even one agent? Obviously the relation of causality is wholly transcended in such a case; and an author has no right to retain the advantage of the suggestion of words which in such an application are utterly eviscerated of their proper meaning.

The same line of remark would apply to the use of the term subject, or conscious subject, or even consciousness. A conscious subject or self identified with a unifying process without a nature to begin with, or for that part to end with, is a remarkable conception. The process of unifying—consciously unifying—is an act of a conscious subject, in as far as it means anything at all. There is the nature of the subject, the act of the subject,—nay, there is even the matter or object dealt with. And when these things are denied to exist, the words implying them are used inappropriately and unjustly, and with the effect of securing an advantage in the discussion which is wholly illegitimate.

But it seems that this unifying process, which to some would hardly appear to be an abstraction, but a simple piece of empty verbalism, gets a meaning for us from the fact that in our action in knowledge there is an instance of the exercise of such causality. Our consciousness, as we are frequently told, is "a reproduction" of that mind or process of unifying, "in respect at least of its attributes of self-origination and unification of the manifold" (p. 82). It has already been shown how absolutely the ground fails here,—that, in fact, there is no such process in our consciousness —that it is merely transferring the so-called conception of this timeless unifying to our experience, without attempting in the least to vindicate the conception from its inherent impossibility. The only reason here adduced for it, as applied to our experience, is stated in these words :—

"A form of consciousness which conceives time cannot, for that reason alone, be in time" (p. 82). Why so? A self conscious of or conceiving time —apprehending succession in time—cannot therefore be in time. Why not? What cogency is there here? Why in that case should it be possible that a form of consciousness which conceives the supposed Eternal Consciousness, yet be, as is alleged, in that Eternal Consciousness? or, much more, be that Eternal Consciousness which it conceives? If it had been said that a consciousness, or conscious subject which conceives time, cannot be time merely, there would have been some sense in the statement. As it stands, it is without proof, and even irrational. If a subject conceives time, his act at least must be in it to the extent that it is the act of the moment in which he conceives it.

The new phrase, "self-origination of the manifold," is quite an addition to the usual "unification." It is another instance of the attempt to unite the conception of a nature and power in the consciousness—ours or the other—with the absence of these things. And it further adds the conception of pure arbitrariness in the self-origination, seeing there is nothing whatever in the way of order to work upon, as there is nothing whatever in the shape of a worker.

In proceeding to his theory of free intelligence, Mr Green makes certain statements or admissions which he thinks necessary steps, but which are hardly consistent with his general doctrine. It seems that "an organism or living body is something in itself other than what its relations make it—that, while it is related to other things according to mechanical and chemical laws, it has itself a nature which is not mechanical or chemical" (p. 85). "But the living body does not, as such, present its nature to itself in consciousness. It does not consciously distinguish itself from its relations. Man, on the other hand, does so distinguish himself. . . . He consciously distinguishes himself from all that happens to him" (p. 85). Man, on this view, is released from the thraldom of organic processes, to be handed over as the subject or vehicle of the reproduction of an Eternal Consciousness—that is, the necessary inexplicable mutual relation of the one and the many, eternally constituted, absolute and unchangeable. Many people would think the one necessity very much on the level of the other. Yet this is human freedom—the ground of obligation and moral ideal.

"In respect of principle, though man is a self, and distinguishes himself as such, he exerts a free activity—an activity which is not in time, not a link in the chain of natural becoming; which has no antecedents other than itself, but is self-originated" (p. 86). The organic processes have a strictly natural history; but there is in man "the action of an Eternal Consciousness, which uses them as its organs, and reproduces itself through them" (p. 86). The organism as in man may be the result of evolution from lower forms of organism, in which the Eternal Consciousness did not reveal or reproduce itself. But this does not affect the doctrine that an eternal consciousness is now implied in human knowledge. There is "an absolute difference between change and the intelligent consciousness or knowledge of change, which precludes us from tracing any development of the one into the other, if development implies any identity of principle between the germ and the developed outcome" (p. 88). But the organism of man in which there is now the eternal intelligence might possibly be-developed through stages of growth and modification in animals, until in man it became the fit vehicle of this intelligence (p. 89). As to the ethical bearing of this metaphysical theory, I do not at present propose to discuss it fully. But I may say that it seems to me that, as the Eternal Consciousness is described by Mr Green, it has not actually or necessarily any moral quality whatever; and accordingly, that its reproduction in man, however far this may proceed or be desired by the individual, can yield no moral ideal whatever. It is simply a self-distinguishing consciousness, in any and every conceived or conceivable object: it is, in fact, the relation or distinction between subject and object. To it every object is indifferent, or indifferently an object, provided only it be an object. It has neither emotion, desire, nor will. It is at the utmost a pure or mere intelligence; and its reproduction in man could at the best lead only to development in knowledge, which is not in the least coextensive, or even identical, with the moral ideal of humanity. In fact, it seems to me that mere self-distinguishing does not imply any end at all —any conception of successive improvement, or of growth towards that perfection which the moral consciousness requires and yearns after.

Motive is, we are told, always an idea of personal good, and the question of moral freedom is the question as to the origin of motives. The self or self-consciousness identifies itself with some desire; this identification is the motive, and the resulting act is therefore free. The motive is not a mere desire, and there is no unmotived desire between motives, neither is the act necessarily determined by the strongest motive. The act does necessarily proceed from the motive; but the motive is not one of the desires which solicit a man, but one of these as identified by the man with himself. That the motive is the outcome of circumstances and character is compatible with the idea of freedom, if it be understood that both circumstances and character, though conditioned, are conditioned only through a self-distinguishing and self-seeking consciousness. But the character of a man is not something other than himself, which co-operates with an equally independent force of circumstances to determine his action. For the character is the man who is thus not determined except as he determines himself. And though the act is a necessary result, the agent is not a necessary because not a natural agent. Remorse and self-reformation are thus intelligible, because action proceeds from self-consciousness, and not from an unmotived power of choice. But if my present depends on my past, and my future on my present, why should I try to become better? This arises from confusedly supposing that if the act is a necessary result of the agent, the agent must be necessary—that is, an instrument of natural forces. But the question implies that the agent is not this, but a self-distinguishing and self-seeking consciousness; that his future depends upon this consciousness, and that it would be absurd to try to become, unless it so depended.—(P. 100 *et seq.*)

The identification of self by itself with a desire —this is moral freedom. Why or how the identification? Not, as the indeterminist supposes, the will making an unmotived choice, but the self determining itself, or freely identifying itself with the desire. This is simply to throw the difficulty as to free choice a step backwards. Why the self should determine itself or identify itself with *this* desire rather than *that*, is no more thus explained than on the theory of indeterminism and motiveless choice. And when we know that this self which seeks and determines itself in this particular mode is really the Eternal Self or consciousness, the whole ground of individuality and possible moral action for man is swept away.

VIII.—THE INFINITE SELF-CONSCIOUSNESS — GENERAL CONSIDERATIONS — SUMMARY.

INSTEAD of the term "Eternal" we find sometimes used that of "Infinite"; and we have ready talk about an or the "Infinite Self-consciousness." The change in the phrase seems to me to be of little moment. It suggests, however, a line of criticism somewhat different from the foregoing.

If this "Infinite Self-consciousness" be more than a mere abstraction — that is, an ideal not restricted to this or that time, or the mere relative in a correlation,—if it be, as is alleged, a reality,—how is it known as such to us? This is the question as to proof.

(1.) Is it known by Intuition—immediately, directly, as we know our modes of mind—ourselves? Do we know in any one intuition a one consciousness which reproduces itself in every finite consciousness in the world? If known as a one universal consciousness, it must be known in one intuition. It cannot be known in parts or succession, and yet known as one. If known in one intuition, it is known as in one moment of time—that is, an infinite self-consciousness is known as existing in a single instant of time, and is known as infinite, and yet under the restriction of a definite instant of time. By intuition, subject to limit, it cannot be known, as infinite, or as the one infinite. Further, as is obvious from the terms, no intuition of the Infinite or Absolute,—taken as Absolute unity, —is possible in human consciousness, unless on the necessary implicate of the identification of the Ego or consciousness with this absolutely one being—this all-comprehending unity.

(2.) Is it known mediately through the data of our experience? by some kind of inference from these data? or sum of data? Is it that we run back the facts, the laws,—the matter and the form of our experience,—to one infinite self-conscious reality, and that we must do so?—these data being the parts or effects or modes of its constant ever-present activity,—manifestations of its being and self-hood. The question here is not regarding a power, analogous to ourselves, behind all, even in all, the root and ground of all, but of a power as an infinite self-consciousness, manifesting itself in all, as finite self-hood manifests itself in the phænomena of mind or consciousness. It is a self-consciousness, but an infinite one. We must claim that people be kept to the meaning of their words. On what ground, then, is it that I infer the fact of an infinite self-consciousness from my experience as knowing and being? I am not aware that any attempt of the least moment has been made to answer this question, or to face the question in any direct way.

To say, as is done, " that thought of any kind, positive or negative, doubting or asserting, postulates itself,—postulates, that is, not the thought of the individual thinker, but a thought of self-consciousness that is prior to all individual thinking, and is the absolute element or atmosphere in which it lives and breathes,"—is the purest begging of the question at issue. It means simply that there is a possibility of abstraction,—of looking at consciousness in general, and considering the individual consciousness as an instance of it. But to regard this as a *prius* of the individual is simply to hypostatise an abstraction, and make that first which is really last. When the necessary link comes to be established, it is not to be done by " postulating."

Why should I regard myself, the matter I

know, the forms of my knowing—the logical and metaphysical laws of knowledge, the generalised laws of science, as the modes or manifestations of a self-conscious being transcending me and my experience, and conscious in me and my experience? Why should I further regard this being as conscious of itself, not only in me, but in every human being or finite ego—nay, in all the realm of being and science? What is there in my conscious experience to lead me to this conclusion? I confess I find nothing adduced of the least relevancy. There is a talk of the need of an infinite self-consciousness as the ground of the relations among objects in the world of knowledge and being. Objects are known in relation —under forms of category—and in relation to a conscious subject. But I do not see how this in any way proves that these relations known to me, or even merely existing relations, if there be such, are the thoughts of an infinite self-consciousness,—that I and all my experience are simply the working, activity, or reproduction of an ego, common to me and to every finite intelligence. Nay, as I find that the relations in question are regarded as essential to the reality of this infinite self-consciousness, that these are reciprocally necessary, I do not see why the relations among things should not be regarded as constituting this infinite self-consciousness, as much, at least, as this self-consciousness can constitute them. The infinite ego is only as it is in relations: the relations are only as in the infinite ego. Then which is which? or what is the difference between them? The one fundamental relation I know is that of subject and object in consciousness. The infinite ego is in this, and this is in the infinite ego. But how, then, am I to distinguish them, and say the ego is first or constitutive? Why may not I equally say, the relation of subject and object is first, and constitutive of the ego? Wherein does such a doctrine differ from the *impression*—the conscious impression, or series of impressions—of Hume, in which subject and object, form and matter, activity and object, are simply fused indiscriminately in one expression?

But it seems to me that this infinite ego is not only not warranted by our consciousness experience. - It actually contradicts it. I do not, as a matter of fact, find that all objects are a part of me, or mode of me or my consciousness. I find a limit, a very marked limit, between me, the conscious and sentient subject, and objects in correlation with me. I find a limit to the sphere of my conscious and sentient being, and I do not find that I can fuse these, or identify them.

I cannot say that all objects I know are permeated by my consciousness or sentiency. I know they are not, or at least I have no reason to say they are. How, then, am I entitled, on the ground of experience, limited and contrasted as it thus is, to say that these two sides of being, though in synthesis, are really only the manifestations of one infinite ego, self-conscious in each? I have nothing in my experience corresponding to this. How, then, on the ground of my experience, can I make such an affirmation?

But further, I cannot reconcile such a conception, if it may be called so, of an infinite ego— one, single, universal—with the reality of me as an ego at all. The essential requirement of my reality as one, single, definite personality, is that of limit, discrimination, contrast, definite distinction, from every other ego. If an ego is, then there are other egos, either real or ideal. But the moment I lose distinctivity, I cease to be an ego, and am merged either in what is a non-ego or in some other ego. But how can I retain limit, distinctivity, if there be but one infinite ego, and I be merely its reproduction, or a manifestation of it?

I say this is inconceivable, impossible; and accordingly you have but two results. Either the infinite ego is, and it is all, every ego, and I am not; or I am—this definite ego or personality, and what I call an infinite ego subsists only in me or as I am conscious. There is thus the choice simply of a pantheistic idealism, which is contradicted by the experience on which it founds, or the infinite ego is a name simply for the human or finite ego. If this latter be real, God is man; if it be taken generically, as the concept or abstraction of the finite ego, God is that abstraction. And this—the identification really or ideally of the infinite with the finite ego—is the alternative chosen by the Hegelian left—the two Bauers, Feuerbach, and Max Stirner.

On this all-important point of the relation of the infinite ego to the finite ego of consciousness, we have no light from Neo-Kantianism. But we ought to get definite answers to these questions:—

(1.) Does the infinite ego or self-consciousness reveal itself to me—the finite ego—in each synthesis of knowledge or consciousness?

If the answer be in the affirmative, then the infinite ego—the universal self—reveals itself to me, the finite self, in a given moment of time, and as existing in a given moment of time. But such a self has and can have no time limitation; and the moment it is subjected to such, it ceases to be the universal, or infinite self or ego.

(2.) Or does the infinite self-consciousness reproduce itself in me—the finite consciousness—each time I know a succession, or know at all? What, then, am I—the finite ego? A reproduction—a ceaseless reproduction of the infinite self-consciousness. And so is every finite human ego. The reproductions will be as numerous as the egos of the universe. Every human organism holds, so to speak, this reproduction. But how can the one infinite ego or self-consciousness reproduce itself in the finite ego, and much more in every finite ego? What becomes of its infinity in the first instance, and what becomes of its unity in the second? Such a theory issues only in its own self-annihilation. The only conceivable being of any finite ego on such a hypothesis is an illusory one. It cannot be an ego truly; it can be only the shadow and the seeming of the one universal self, which gleams for a moment in our organism, and then passes on. We may conserve the organism in such a case; we do not conserve the ego—either self-hood or personality.

Further, is the reproduction of the infinite self-consciousness, as a power or reality in the finite, compatible with any contingency of fact to be met with in experience? It is regarded as a creative, or at least constitutive, power, working out the world of experience; it has reality only as it does this, and as it is in the world of experience. Could this world, then, have been anything else than it is as an existence or matter of fact, on such a supposition? If the order of experience known to us be only, as it is, the manifestation of an infinite self-consciousness, and this self-consciousness be only as it is revealed in or creates the known world of existence, how is the contingency of such a world even conceivable? To attribute contingency to it, or the possibility of being other than it is, is to contradict the very supposition from which we start. But if this be so, what are the logical results? The present or known order of things, and things as we know them on this planet, and as far as we can know them elsewhere, or the infinite self-consciousness can know them through us, which is quite the same thing, is the only possible, and it is necessary. Everything is exactly as it may be, and as it must be. But there are opposites, even contradictions, in this experience of ours—this manifested, created, necessary experience of the infinite self-consciousness. There is, for example, the known contrast of finite subject and object in knowledge and reality; there is the contrast of the evil motive and deed with the virtuous motive and deed; there is the contrast of this individual and that individual: but all this is equally the manifestation or creation of the one infinite self-consciousness; in this even, and only in this, it is. It is manifest in all, and it is one; it is universal, it is infinite. What, then, becomes of the very idea of opposition or contradiction in experience; of the opposition of subject and object in the one individual; of the opposition of good and evil in experience; of pleasure and pain; of the opposition of the multiplicity of individual egos; of the plurality of the race of mankind? The very idea of opposition is sapped. The thing is an illusion; all is only the manifestation,—the creation,—of the one infinite universal self-consciousness, which is at the root of things and is in things; and all opposition is a simple illusion to be dispelled by this higher reason,—this new light on the universe of God. If we hold by the supposition of the self-manifesting, infinite, universal self-consciousness, then all in the world—all the manifested or existent, however different to us or in appearance—is really the same in essence, in ultimate reality or fact; or if we hold by the difference—the oppositions of experience—there is no ultimate one self-consciousness, or being with a unity of nature so related to this world of ours.

If by one infinite self-consciousness at the root

of things is meant an energy or act of power, reason and will, whose beginning we cannot know or fix, which even lies at the root of the two possibilities of finite being — time and space — is now, and shall for ever be, working in and through things, in all the development of the world and man—in its being and upholding,— then I should say this seems to me a necessity of the case. But I should think this exceedingly ill, indeed misleadingly, described as one infinite self-consciousness, because this would actually contradict certain of its own known results. It would further be exceedingly unworthily described as an eternal energy in the sense of being a single determinate necessary outgoing of a power, grounding the energy. This would be unworthy also of certain of its results, and could give us no free power or ethic worthy of the name. A spiritual free power at the root of things, in things now, conditioning all — the background of all—that I can take as a conception grounded on the highest analogy of my own experience, but only as a result grounded on psychological and ethical facts, and on science or the reigning order of the outward world. How perfectly to construe it to my mind, how to relate it precisely to the finite world, that I do not profess to know.

But it may very fairly be argued that the contradictions involved in the terms used are such as to destroy the whole theory. In other words, the theory is not only not proved, it cannot be stated consistently in terms.

Is the notion of self — a conscious self — compatible with "infinite," in any sense of the word?

Self is a definite individual conscious reality. Only as such, and thus distinguished from other selves, material and spiritual, is it a reality at all. An *infinite* self may mean a self not limited or limitless,—as an infinite space or an infinite time. Is this limitlessness compatible with the notion of self at all? If self have no limit, how is it self? Is that which is absolutely without bounds anything but a form of indefinite possibility? It may mean a self capable of *infinite* development, in time and in space—a development without limit on any side or form. This development would be a manifestation, and there would thus be constant or everlasting ongoing or process of manifestation. But if this development stopped, it would not be describable as an infinite but a finite self. It would never, therefore, be at any time an infinite self, but only a self on its way to the infinite. As a self capable of infinite development, it would be capable of development not only through all time and space, but through everything in time and space, would indeed develop the things in time and space, both their matter and their form; for anything, either matter or form, out of the development, would limit it. And this infinite self, being conscious or self-conscious, would be conscious of itself as in its development. It would thus be conscious of all that is—matter and form—as itself, or at least a mode of itself, contained in its being. This would be the gradual realisation of the all-creating, all-embracing soul of the universe. The ultimate goal of such an infinite would be the permeating of the world as an organism, in which this self rose to infinite self-consciousness. As in our own bodily organism, we are conscious and sentient all through; so this self would finally realise itself in the full permeation, so to speak, of all the contents of space and time. But such a self-consciousness is a growth, and ought not to be spoken of in the beginning as an infinite self-consciousness, but as something on the way to this stage.

Further, this infinite self-consciousness is reproduced in me and in all other individual self-consciousnesses. We are part of its creation and development. Is it a complete reproduction of itself? Then in this case there will be as many infinite self-consciousnesses as there are finite egos in the universe, and the unity of self-consciousness is a dream. Is it only a partial reproduction, thus finite or limited in each and by each? Then what becomes of its unity—thus broken up and disintegrated? And how am I to know in this case that there is one infinite self-consciousness?

Further, does my consciousness of myself in experience necessitate a reference, either of correlation or of implication, to an infinite self-consciousness, as a reality on which I depend, and which is necessary to my being conscious of myself? My consciousness of myself implies, as correlative, something distinguished from me, either a passing mode of consciousness, or a perceived quality of the outer world. As actual, my self-consciousness implies the reality of the mode or quality perceived; as conceptional, the conception of the mode or quality perceived. But it in no way necessitates me to think one infinite self-consciousness, or a self-consciousness extending through all time and space and things. On the contrary, it excludes this; and in affirming itself as a self, one, indivisible, denies any one infinite self-consciousness known to me, both the mind and the world.

I may think of a self-consciousness as embodying the conception and form of my own self-consciousness. This would be a simple abstraction from my experience of myself as myself. But it would not necessarily have any reality; it would be simply the individual (logical) which I form in order to embody or realise the notion of self-consciousness. If I made this more than a logical individual—a real, numerical individual—I should personify or hypostatise the object of an abstraction. And if I added to it the epithet "infinite," because it is realisable in every actual and conceivable self-consciousness, I should mistake the logical universality of the concept for an individual of real existence. If by "infinite" I meant "limitless," or capable of indefinite development, I should fall into the contradictions and absurdities already indicated. And this apotheosis of an abstraction is really what is implied in the theory. The universal is purely logical; it is the common element in knowledge, generalised, universalised. This is truly what is meant by "a pure ego"; but such a conception is utterly unthinkable *per se*, just as any other concept is: it has existence neither in thought nor in reality; and the realising of it, or the individualising of it, is simply the act of a finite self-consciousness, which thinks or imagines itself knowing. But this abstract in no way constitutes the finite ego; the finite ego constitutes it.

Further, an infinite self-consciousness may be a misnomer for an eternal self-consciousness,—meaning an act out of and above time or succession altogether. How this has got any connection with development and relations,—relations making up the world—the world of time and space,—it is hard to see. An eternal act, or an eternal anything that never comes into time at all, or comes in altogether, in one indivisible moment, thus flashing out all relations, all reality, at once, is a conception, if it can be called such, which has no bearing whatever on our experience, or any experience conceivable by us, which is necessarily a time-experience—a continuous development. As a theory not only transcendental but absolutely transcendent of thought, fact, time, it may be left to the mid-air position of Mahomet's coffin—never getting to heaven, and never touching earth.

The theory of which I have been speaking seems to me to be founded—

(1.) On the idea of a real self or ego, which it gets in experience or empirical consciousness.

(2.) It regards this self as a universal, or universal individual, still retaining the idea of its reality.

(3.) It regards the universal or infinite self as the power which manifests all that is,—subject and object—mind and the world.

(4.) At the same time, it denies the universal self anything but an actual reality, as in its manifestations of subject and object—mind and the world. It thus falls back into the view of the inseparable synthesis of the one and the many, as constituting the only reality. It ceases, therefore, to explain the synthesis as the result of a real self, or potency, at the cost of things, and is content to say the synthesis is all that is.

(5.) It thus saps the very conception of constituting relationship; for as the terms are really inseparable, only exist as related, there could never have been a point at which, or from which, the relationship was constituted.

(6.) We can form no conception of any relation unless between a plurality of terms: in particular, there can be no unifying by us, or in our conception, unless as we are conscious of the different, or manifold, to be unified. But no provision is made for a plurality of terms,—this plurality is even denied: in particular, there is no possibility of a consciousness of the manifold unless as already related to the one; and hence there can be no unifying, no synthesis, no putting together, in any natural sense of the terms.

It thus seems to me that in those positions there is a hopeless contradiction. This arises ultimately from the attempt to grasp the totality of the world in a single conception; whereas the facts alike of man and nature are incompatible with any such conception. The two incompatible ideas in the theory of a universal self are those of constitution by the self—implying reality *per se* and potential existence—in fact, freedom; and the conception of the reality of the self as in, and only in, the manifestation. These two conceptions we cannot reconcile. We must give up constitution with the surrender of reality *per se*. All that is left to us after that is process—ongoing, unaccountable process—or, rather, the law and mode of development, at least, of ongoing; not even the one passing into the many, but the simple interlacing of one and many—the iron band that subsists amid the passing materials. This, so far from corresponding to the idea of God, does not imply spirituality at all—not even intelligence, far less freedom. All that it amounts to is that there is an order in things, but an order observed by the things themselves. And we can say no more about it. Causality, potency, creative power, are utterly given up. To say that the world must be many and one, is to tell me nothing about the origin or genesis of the world, or even about the actual contents of the world which are thus uniform and manifold; and it is to tell me nothing about the cause or causality, either before the world or in the world. This abandonment of causality and the elevation of mode or law to its place, called relation, is the annihilation of even the possibility of the question—What is the Supreme Power at work in the world? Pantheistic Idealism, in its most recent form, and Comtism, as equally excluding cause from things, and substituting law or sequence, seem to me thus to be, as far as theistic result is concerned, undistinguishable.

What are the objections, it may be asked, to the scheme of a Deity or Supreme Power, above nature and finite Mind, distinct from these really and numerically, yet related to them as cause, as free cause or power — that is, a God conceived as conscious Will and Intelligence, after the highest form of causality we know?

These are—(*a*) that such a relation between God and the world involves a "dualism," and "philosophy" seeks necessarily a unity, a monism, as the explanation of things; (*b*) that such a relation is "accidental," "external," "arbitrary," thus contingent. We must, in a word, have a cause which, from its nature, must pass into the world, and show its nature in the world, or through the nature of the world.

Now as to the phrase about "dualism," I set not the slightest store by it. There may be dualism in the universe, or there may not. But to assume that there must be monism, and that ultimately philosophy must find the one, otherwise it is not "philosophy," is simply to make a wholly gratuitous assumption, and to peril the existence of philosophy on a condition that may never be realised. What philosophy seeks, and ought to seek, is something higher even than monism, and that is the truth, the ultimate truth of things. Whether this be monism, spiritual or material, for the latter would equally well satisfy the requirement of unity, or whether it be dualism, or that which we can only name as such, is a matter to be settled by philosophy; but the settlement one way or another, whether monistic or dualistic, would not be suicide for philosophy itself.

As to the phrases "external," "accidental," "arbitrary," they really are without force or relevancy. Supposing the world to be an act of the Divine, the result of a free act not necessitated, this would be no more "arbitrary," "accidental," "external" to His Being, than an act of free-will is to ours. As I have said elsewhere, "so far from a creation which depends on an act of free-will, regulated by thought analogous to our experience, evidencing only an external or accidental relationship, it is in fact the symbol of the very closest, most intimate, of all the relationships of our consciousness. For the closest tie which we know in our inward experience is just that which subsists between the *willing* and the *resolution* which I form. I relate resolution to myself in a way in which I relate no other mode of consciousness, either feeling, desire, or thought itself. It is mine in the sense of being truly my own creation; and it is to me the most fitting of all analogies for the mysterious fact of Divine origination itself. The finite, as thus related to the infinite, is truly the passage of the Divine Power into actuality or realisation. It is only a purely verbal logic, founding on verbal assumptions, which can regard it as 'external' or 'accidental.' . . . Will, the expression of personality, both as originating resolutions and moulding existing material into form, is the nearest approach in thought which we can make to Divine Creation."[1]

But, further, what is the alternative given to

---

[1] Descartes, *Introduction*, pp. clxv, clxvi.

us here? The cause must be such, that from its nature it must pass into act, and so manifest its nature.

In the first place, the cause, call it infinite or absolute, is under a necessity of manifestation. Well, then, the development will be in one definite form, and no other. Necessity knows no variation. The development is in time; let us take it as the development we know, or as has happened, though that we never could predict. But let us take it so. Then our world is the one possible, because it is the one necessary. Are we prepared to take this consequence? Do the facts of experience warrant it? Does the physical or moral quality of the world warrant it? Can we ascribe to the finite material world which we find in our experience more than a purely hypothetical necessity? No one, I think, will venture rationally to do more than this. Mechanical and chemical laws depend ultimately on atomic existence, proportion, combination, collocation. Organisation and life are also somehow connected with those circumstances. But is it not conceivable that those ultimate constituents of the universe might have been different in various points of constitution and adjustment? Will it be maintained that the actual order which we know has arisen is the only possible order—the single necessary and essential development at the root of things? Is there not presumption of the worst and rashest sort in saying that the contents and the laws of this planet of ours, and of such other parts of the universe as we happen to know, is the only possible — the necessary development of the one Infinite Power at the root of Being? Did the necessary development of this power only begin when this planet was cast off from the sun, and commenced existence as a seething mass of matter? And is such necessary development limited to this temporary, passing, isolated world of ours? Further, does not the element of evil in the world imply a contingency which is entirely incompatible with the supposition of a single possible best evolution from an absolutely perfect infinite?[1]

But is the finite being or development not variable in content at the will—the reasonable or righteous will, it may be—of the Infinite One? Then what becomes of his infinity? Can we conceive a Being as infinite who is restricted to a single development of finite being? But if he is not so restricted, but may evolve several forms of finitude, how can it be said that any finite as a given form is necessary to him, or results neces-

[1] Descartes, *Introduction*, p. clxvii.

sarily from his nature? Or, in other words, that he stands in necessary relation to any given development? or to any development which he may not vary—that is, to any development at all? Is not a Power—a personality—which can vary—can control its own development—higher than a Power which is under necessitation in a definite mode?

In the whole, or nearly the whole, of those absolute or transcendental starting-points there is an assumption which is unwarrantable, and really vitiates the whole of the deduction, whether of knowledge or being, in each case. I should express this assumption by saying that there is an abstraction—an undue abstraction—of the actual or real or material side of knowing from the possible, indefinite, or formal side. To understand this we may start, in the first place, from what every one acknowledges—"I think," "I am conscious," "I know." In so expressing ourselves we use two terms — that which thinks, that which is conscious, or, if you choose, that which comes to think, that which comes to consciousness. Now, which is the ultimate here —if ultimate there be, or be sought? Is it that which thinks, or is it the thinking? Our philosophy will be determined almost wholly by the answer which we give to this question—by the alternative which we select.

What is Kant's alternative? Apparently the thinking, the consciousness, but the pure or mere consciousness—that is, the consciousness viewed abstractly from that which is conscious. It is in his language the synthetic unity of apperception or consciousness. This is an act or process, if it have any meaning at all. It is the consciousness, not that which is conscious or comes to consciousness. It is the thinking, not the "I." And out of this pure or mere consciousness, if so much can be credited to it, the "I" of consciousness comes. In fact, the order, the logical order, is reversed. It is not I who think or am conscious who generates or is the source of consciousness, but it is the consciousness, the pure, mere abstract consciousness, which so to speak, generates the "I" or "me." This, it seems to me, is the fruitful source of the aberrations in method of subsequent German transcendentalism — of the systems of Fichte, Schelling, and Hegel. With Fichte for Kant's phrase is substituted the "pure ego," but this is no more that which thinks than it is with Kant. It means with Fichte, and can only mean on a system which states a basis above experience, "pure thought" or "pure consciousness" divorced from an actual ego, but issuing in it afterwards, as it issues in nature. With Schelling, also, the indifference or identity of subject and object is not that which thinks the identity, but the consciousness, real or supposed, of the identity itself. And with Hegel we have the most obvious acknowledgment of the separation of the pure consciousness or being from that which is conscious; in the Idea, as equivalent to the Real, in pure thought—pure being; as the principle of all, as in and constituting all, developing through all, through finite mind or Ego, Nature, up to Absolute Idea.

Now I say this is a wholly illegitimate and illogical abstraction. If you are to seek an ultimate being beyond the me thinking or consciousness, it is not the consciousness or thinking on which you ought to fix, but on that which every conceivable act of consciousness or concept even of consciousness presupposes—viz., that which is conscious, and which knows itself to be conscious. Pure or mere consciousness is not the first thing, relatively, but the "I" or thinker. Pure or mere thinking has no meaning, or conceivability even, apart from that which underlies it. Nay, such a concept has no power of movement, or of doing anything whatever. It has no dynamic in itself, and it is only as that which thinks, moves, acts,—that it can move or act, or come into any form of conceivable reality or fact. It will be found that the alternative which holds to both the ego and the consciousness as the primordial fact in knowledge at least, is the true one, whether we regard the ego as constitutive of knowledge or merely the observer of the great spectacle of things.

It might easily be shown that the same form of fallacious basis runs through the system as in Plato, which would make idea the first and formative—that is, idea *per se*. We can form no conception of such a process, apart from that which ideates, so to speak, and realises the idea. Call your forms idea, apperception, category, concept, pure consciousness, pure thought, call it what you will,—this is, after all, an abstraction, and an illegitimate abstraction, which puts the second first, and which is utterly powerless to take a single step into the sphere of being.[1]

On the grounds which I have stated, and others which might be adduced, I think the theory of a literal one infinite self-consciousness which I have now noticed quite untenable, and fitted to throw no light on the problem of the world, either as to origin, character, or destiny, or on the same points touching man. Such a theory, moreover, proceeds on a false or unsound philo-

---

[1] Cf. Descartes, *Introduction*, chapters iii., iv., xi., xii.; and later, Bax, *History of Philosophy*, p. 345.

sophical method. It begins at the wrong end; and though it professes to keep in view always experience, or its possibility, it wholly loses sight of the relevant facts.

The true method, as seems to me, is—

(1.) To accept and start from our own finite self-consciousness, our own definite reality as personality, as self-hood, guaranteed to us in experience and the necessity of thought.

(2.) To show that all knowledge whatever, and therefore every object of knowledge, is in relation to this—the real, definite, conscious subject; and this would include the knowledge even, the alleged knowledge, of an infinite self-consciousness.

(3.) That to subvert the finite self-consciousness is to subvert all knowledge. Unless this be indubitable, nothing else is certain. To make it illusory is to make all knowledge illusory—to sap, in a word, the foundations of realism, idealism, infinite egoism itself.

(4.) To show that, with the finite ego of consciousness as a basis, we may, nay, perhaps must, rise above it, to an ego in the world—spiritual, like our ego knowing; free, like our ego willing; creative, like our ego doing,—known thus not anthropomorphically, but by analogy, with what is highest in our conscious experience. And this higher ego can, I think, be best reached through the argument of dependence, or the broken, incomplete, imperfect character of our experience, as in man and the world. This would be to ground on a fact, not to hypostatise an abstraction.

The main fallacy which runs all through the reasoning of the school to which I have referred, is supposing that in what is called the transcendental proof or deduction of the elements of knowledge, we can deal with any knowledge other than the human, with knowledge in general, or that we can have any higher guarantee for any assertion whatever than the necessity which lies in the thought of each individual, testing it for himself. No man can do more than analyse his own conscious knowledge, which exists as a fact, into its elements; and he can have no other or higher guarantee for the *nexus* or connection of those elements than the necessity he feels of thinking it, either directly, or indirectly, through the necessity of foregoing principles. Even if I come to allege the necessity of the one infinite self-consciousness as at the root of all, this after all is but a conviction in me, the individual thinker, which I hold and believe to be necessary. After all, the one infinite self-consciousness hangs on my thinking, and it is the merest delusion to suppose that because I call it by this high-sounding name, it can possibly have any guarantee beyond the ordinary psychological analysis and reflection; and this, when rightly interpreted, only exposes its inconsistency and its emptiness.

The other fallacy in the method seems to me to consist in making the universal ego necessary to knowledge, a reality or power capable of manifesting itself, even creating things, while it is a simple abstraction from the fact that in all our knowledge there is an ego. This is wholly to mistake the nature of an abstraction or abstract idea. The universal ego as an idea has no power or reality in time whatever—no activity. It is on the same level as any concept, which we hold and can realise, by thinking it as exemplified in an instance—in this case, this or that ego. So far from such an ego being a power of creating us, we are the power which creates it—first by abstraction, and then by imagination realising the abstraction. A more complete case of what we call ὕστερον πρότερον cannot be conceived. In this sense, no doubt, a universal ego is intelligible; but it is wholly powerless, wholly useless as a ground of reality.

Further, I may add that I do not see how even the term God or Deity can be retained on such a theory. When we speak of God, of man,

THE INFINITE SELF-CONSCIOUSNESS. 299

of the world, we mean a contrast—a certain opposition.[1] The two latter may be fused, as it were; they may be regarded as one—a form of finite reality. Still this reality is regarded as different from, even in opposition to, the reality we name God. The term God marks for us the highest reach of opposition in infinite and finite, absolute and relative, unconditioned and conditioned, and other expressions. But, according to the theory, this opposition no longer truly exists in any form, either in knowledge or in reality. The knowledge of the one term, the infinite, is not possible without the knowledge of the other; the reality of the one term is not possible apart from the reality of the other: the one only is as the other is; the other is only as the one is. The terms infinite and finite no longer mark a contrast, but a unity—a unity of knowledge and being. How, then, can the term GOD be any longer applied to that in which He is not distinguished from His opposite, but really fused with it—made dependent on it for His reality? That which is only, as it is one and many, cannot certainly be regarded as the one in the relation. He cannot even be regarded as that which relates the many to the one; He is simply a form of abstract relation-

[1] See Descartes, *Introduction*, p. clxxi *et seq.* Cf. Bax, *History of Philosophy*, p. 393.

ship in which opposition is unknown—a void and empty conception indifferent to content—capable of being spoken of neither as one nor many, neither as reality nor person; above predication, because above attributes, either of power, intelligence, or goodness. God is now neither substance, cause, nor being; He is not the ultimate or the first. What we call God on such a system is as much subject to the iron fate of the relationship, as the minutest particle of being or the meanest of His creatures. The eternal, ever-manifesting relationship of the one and the many is THE SUPREME, and to it the actual one is as indifferent as the many, the many as the one.

IX.—PHILOSOPHY OF RELIGION.

We have treatises professing to deal with the "Philosophy of Religion." The title is an aspiring one. Under the heading "Philosophy of Religion" should be found, in the first place, a broad-minded effort to grasp the religious facts in their integrity and totality, as the religious consciousness and its history present them. Instead of this we have usually placed in the fore-front of the investigation, or to be found running through the discussion, a certain philosophical theory, which is used as the standard by which to try the facts; and simply because these facts do not suit the theory—that is, it may be, because the theory is too narrow for the facts—these are either rejected, or so eviscerated of meaning as to cease to be what they were formerly regarded. And it may possibly be found that the pretensions of the theory put forward are such as cannot be admitted in any science or system of knowledge that deals with the facts of experience. It may be found that these pretensions are applicable only to the line of mathematical reasoning, that they are such as must fail in regard to matter of fact—real, moral, or spiritual,—that even if they could be applied to the abstract categories of thought, they would still leave out all actual reality of time and space and experience in general.

We are told that true knowledge, rational knowledge—that is, philosophical knowledge—is a cognition of necessary truths,—and this in the sense of finding necessary links in all parts of knowledge from beginning to end, so that one is involved in and flows out of the other in an ordered and perfectly necessary systematic connection. We do not find merely that things are, but we discover that they must be, I presume, as they are. The one being given, the others follow, and the whole body of knowledge constitutes one organic system. This is the language of the commentators and followers of Hegel from Vera onwards to recent productions in the same line. We are always to get "systematic," "organised," "rational" knowledge. This is a very fine and high-sounding formula; and we have had pretensions before to mathematical demonstration in philosophical knowledge. In the past, these professions have come to very little; they are not more profitable now. If, instead of standing on this high *a priori* platform—for it is nothing else —the professors would come to experience,—to science with the whole body of its generalisations, to the elements of matter in the form of atoms, and show how these are actually necessarily connected, they would do some relevant and crucial work. If they would further show the necessary transition from atomism, or any stage they may name, to organism and life, and from life to soul and man, and from man to God, they would do something to the purpose and in the way of proving their sounding thesis. But until this is done with some reasonableness and cogency, we may fairly disregard the pretension. Meanwhile, what may be said about the pretension is, that there is no proof or even possibility of showing necessary connections between the truths of science from the beginning to the end, even the widest generalisations of science, that such a series of necessary links could apply to the abstract categories of thought alone, that these links have not been supplied in regard even to them, and that if they were supplied, the system would still leave out of sight the whole world of individual realities,—all that is of highest concern to us, all that is most worthy of attention in any system of philosophy deserving the name.

But, further, there must be straightforward intellectual dealing with this "thought," "organic reason," or whatever it may be called, in which Man, Nature, God are both moments, which is the unity of all, and which I am said to get as a presupposition of my self-consciousness,—consciousness of subject and object in experience. We ought to be frankly told whether it is simply an "other" of me and my self-consciousness,—a higher, larger self,—the "thought" I know and am—a reduplication, in a word, of my self-consciousness. But this apparently is not so, for thus we should not escape the much-decried theory of anthropomorphism, and we should retain the laws and limitations which are essential to finite thought and constitute it. What, then, we have to ask, is "the thought" or "reason" which is the necessary postulate of our thought or reason? What is that "thought" in which we are, and nature is, and which is also God? It is clearly not our thought, nor anything in the least like our thought; for our thought, as is admitted in phrases calling it "the logical understanding," "the finite consciousness," and so on, is subject to the laws which regulate definite knowledge—intuition and conception,—the laws of Identity and Non-Contradiction, without which a definite object is neither conceivable nor intelligible,—without which the definite intuition of an object in time or in time and space, suffers complete dissolution,—without which, in a word, the absurd is all-pervading, and knowledge chaos. This is the limitation,—the essential constitution of our thought,—its very nerve and sinew. The identity of an intuition with itself, the self identity of the point of time or space in which the perception occurs, the distinction of the before and the after in all intuitional knowledge, the identity of a definite concept with itself, the absolute exclusion of intuition and concept from its contradictory sphere, the opposition of the fixed concept, scientific or moral, to its contradictory negative,—all this is guaranteed to us by the laws of Identity and Non-Contradiction; and if these are abolished or suspended, our knowledge, our thought, is abolished, and we have in its place pure meaninglessness,—the deceptive shadow of knowledge in the formulas of empty words. But "the thought" which, wonderfully enough, "our thought" postulates as its necessary presupposition, is the very reverse of all this. This other thought or reason, it seems, seeks unity—complete unity; and unity is not to be got by mere affirmation that a thing is what it is,—as if, by the way, any one ever said that affirmation under logical law did more than declare and preserve unity. This higher or other thought is a thought or conception, if we may still retain the words in their new and unusual application, which runs what a thing is into what it is not,—affirmation into negation, existence by itself into existence other than itself,—into a denial which gives up any separate self-identical being or life. And it does all this in order to reach unity—true unity—the being of the thing as it is, as at once what is and is not. This is the presupposition of our limited and conditioned thought, and it works in the spheres of Nature, Man, and God, fuses them, takes them up into itself, and so constitutes the universe of Being in its totality and its oneness. Thus Man, Nature, and God are in the end reconciled, and the expression "I am *that* I *am*" becomes "I am *that* I am *not*." Various difficulties suggest themselves here, but for the present purpose it is not necessary to ask more than this—Can this "thought," this "reason," be called thought or reason as known to us, or in our consciousness? Are we not now using the word in a wholly new connotation? And have we a right to use it? I say we have not. If thought is to be stripped of its acknowledged law and limitation—that which is its recognised essence—let us coin another word for the supposed entity so designated. We ought to give up the name when we have abandoned the thing.

This "absolute thought" or "reason" is not thought or reason in any sense of the terms. It is not a postulate or presupposition of our conciousness in any form—it is the contradiction of our thought. It does not truly contain relations, for it has nothing to relate; it provides for no ground of relation in any self-existing unity, either time or thought-identity. It has no real unity; it is only as it is in varied relations, and these are only as in it; it is a pure abstraction which has no counterpart in any concrete; it is kept afloat only by unanalysed metaphors and bad analogies.

A complete or reasoned-out system of this world—Man, Nature, and God—is an impossibility on the conditions of our thought, much more on their subversion. "Reason," Hegel tells us, "is Substance as well as Infinite Power. Its own infinite material underlies all the natural and spiritual life which it originates, as also the infinite form,—that which sets this material in motion. On the one hand, Reason is the substance of the universe,—that by which and in which all reality has its being and substance. On the other hand, it is the infinite energy of the universe; since Reason is not so powerless as to be incapable of producing anything but a mere ideal, a mere intention—having its place outside reality, nobody knows where,—something separate and abstract in the heads of certain human beings. It is the infinite complex of things,—their entire essence and truth. It is its own material which it commits to its own active energy to work up. . . . It supplies its own nourishment, and is the object of its own operations. While it is exclusively its own basis of existence, and absolute final aim, it is also the energising power realising this aim, developing it not only in the phænomena of the natural, but also of the spiritual universe—the History of the World. This 'Idea' or 'Reason' is the true, the eternal, the absolutely powerful essence; it reveals itself in the world."[1]

Now I shall take this passage as summary and typical, and I would ask, in the face of it, for an explicit answer to the question as to what finite "reality" in any form can mean, consistently with its averments? In what sense distinctiveness, independence, and difference can be ascribed to the finite self-consciousness, to the Individual Being of time, or of time and space? I would ask further, what possibly can be meant on such a statement by the words Finite Power and Freedom,—by Obligation, Responsibility, the distinctions of Right and Wrong, the law of Duty? I would ask further, even, what is meant by the

[1] Hegel, *History of Philosophy*, pp. 9, 10 (Eng. ed.)

World of Nature,—by the natural and the supernatural, by the material and the spiritual, the human and the divine? These distinctions are said to be preserved " within the Reason." I ask how they are or can be so preserved? I ask also how the development of that which is at once Substance and Power is compatible with the merit and demerit of the actors in history, as all history is simply its manifestation? I ask, in a word, how on such a doctrine anything which is can be anything except that which *must* be? And if so, how that is compatible with any conviction which we possess regarding the possibility of freedom in the realisation by us of moral ends, or the spontaneous homage of worship to a God? These are questions on which I should humbly desire to find some light thrown by those who professedly accept the theory, and yet, as I assume, hold by the realities and possibilities which I challenge as incompatible.

"Moments within the Reason"—this is the expression for the reality of Man, Nature,—all the individualities of the universe,—nay, all the generalities of being. As nothing is fixed on the scheme, and all is flowing, a "moment" even is something. But I fear that a "moment" in the course of the out-going of "the Absolute Reason" —whatever that may be—is not much to help us.

It may appear to have a character of its own for the time, but then this simply comes to become —to pass away into its opposite. Alas for the individual, on the low level of time, who accepts and believes in it! This moment is no more different from the Absolute Substance or Reason than is the drop of water from the stream. It is but one of one and many. And however the sparkle of the moment may make it seem to differ, it is really the same,—only a phase of the passing substantial absolute, which is the law of the identity of all things,—the synthesis of all contradictions. The natural outcome of the Hegelian conception on what may be called its abstract side is simply that the individual is a "reflection,"—the passing reflection of the all-comprehending substance. This side has been actually developed and is represented by Strauss. The absolute is the flow of the individuals of time and space,—thought is the thought of conscious individuals,—the sum of natural law is the divine. On the other hand, as the individual contains the abstract universality, and gives it meaning and being, the supreme principle or ground of all is simply a projection of the likeness of the individual himself on the mirror of his own consciousness. This we have in Feuerbach.[1]

[1] Cf. Descartes, *Introduction*, § xii., and Bax, *History of Philosophy*, p. 341.

Can there be any result of this speculative system but absolute individualism, if anything real be preserved from it at all? What are "the moments" of the absolute Reason on such a view but simply the abstractions which I, the individual, make? How can they have even meaning unless for *me* or some individual in time? And each moment,—what I call man, subjective and objective mind, nature,—mechanical, chemical, organic,—these are all but points of view of mine,—these are abstractions dependent on my individual thought,—ay, and the Reason itself,—the absolute, the God who is the synthesis of all contradictions,—He too is my creation. How then could this grand Monism come to anything but the most isolated Monadism? Certainly nothing else. I have projected from myself certain abstractions, with these I have overshadowed myself, and perhaps I cower under them as objects hypostatised superior to myself. But after all, they are but my own creations. I soon come to find that this is so, and when I give them up as realities I get rid of a domineering and desolating Pantheism. But I have no other refuge except the other alternative of the theory—that of absolute individualism as the basis and ground of all the abstractions which I have been told was the sphere of reality, but which I find is only the realm of shades.

"The surrender of individual ethics" is the last result of Hegelianism, and in its place we are to have social ethics,—that of the family, the city, and the state. The surrender is not only of all individual ethics, but of every ethical conception whatever. And we are no longer to worship an anthropomorphic Deity. No; we are only to worship the absolute, which is the self-conscious synthesis of all contradictions. For my part, though not restricted to that, I prefer the anthropomorphic Deity. If he is not divine, he is at least human.

Perhaps it may be found that the theorising of religion is not quite within the purely speculative or cognitive point of view, and that a philosophy which starts simply from what is called "Reason," or "pure knowledge," or "pure thought," has set out on a wrong track, and not recognising the full or normal nature of man in relation to the universe or whole of experience with what it implies, can but work out the microcosm,—the little world of individual conception, as opposed to the great world,—the macrocosm of God.

The misconceptions about the laws of Identity, and Non-Contradiction being applicable in one sphere and transcended in another, which form the groundwork of most recent Neo-Kantian treatises on religion, are really marvellous to any one ordinarily familiar with what these laws mean. These laws are simply applicable to definite percepts or concepts; they cannot be applied to the indefinite or indeterminate from their very nature, and they are purely hypothetical. Given a percept or concept of that which I definitely know, this is to be regarded as what it is, and not to be identified or confounded with its opposite. The *yellow* I see is not *red* or *blue*, the *organised* I conceive is not the *unorganised* or *inorganic*, the *round* is not the *square*—and so on. We can make no assertion, lay down no premiss, take no step in reasoning, without the assumption here involved. Even when professing to assail the assumption itself, we must make this very assumption: Given A, whatever definite thing it may be, it is not not-A. Such a statement can never be contradicted in a so-called other or higher sphere of knowledge—that is, in the indefinite or indeterminate; for as there is no longer a definite datum to begin with, the law which conserves the identity of the datum with itself has no possibility of application. It cannot conserve what is not as yet definite, for there is nothing to conserve. If the thought be definite to which the law is applied, it is absolute, insuperable, for it is wholly relative to the difference between the thought and its opposite: if the so-called thought be indefinite, the law has no application except such as is possible terminally. There is, therefore, no possibility of such a law being valid in one sphere and not in another.

Then, further, such a law applies even to the definite only hypothetically. The datum is to be somehow got or given—something is—ere the law can come into application at all. Then we can predicate of it self-identity. The relationship is therefore hypothetical; and, as such, is incapable of categorical denial. This makes it always absolute or insuperable. Except in the sphere of the given datum, the relation cannot hold, and cannot be either true or false. It cannot, therefore, be subverted in any sphere of intelligibility whatever—called reason or anything else—and much less can such a principle be made a means of method or immanent dialectic in developing the indeterminate through its negation to definite content.

Another fruitful source of confusion in this subject is the lack of a clear and precise conception of what "externality" means, as applied to the space-world, to other selves, and to Deity Himself. This involves the whole question of independent existence. As to the world in space, externality is used and spoken of by some writers as if the relation involved were a purely space-relation—that is, of points out of points — the relation exemplified in space itself. Consciousness or the self-conscious is, as it were, set up here in this point of space, and externality is assumed to mean other things there in space. There is talk of the *outside* of consciousness, as if consciousness were regarded as a sort of pitcher with a proper locality in space, and some things might be inside it and other things outside it. This is pretty much the Neo-Kantian representation of the realistic view of consciousness. And we are told that there is no "outside" of consciousness—all is inside; all is inside, or rather if there be an outside, there is no outside *to* consciousness; it is always an outside *in* consciousness. The inside of consciousness contains insides and outsides, but it has no outside to itself. The principle of the "stick argument" seems to be here for the moment forgotten—that an inside implies an outside, just as the one end of the stick implies the other.

The true conception of internality and externality has nothing to do with trifling verbalism of this sort. That is said to be internal, or within the mind, which is a property or quality of the mind or ego,—as feeling, perceiving, remembering, reasoning, willing. These are in the mind as the subject of inherence,—as its special constitutive properties. They with the ego are internal, whatever be the relation of the ego to time or space. They constitute the manifested internal reality of mind, as opposed to qualities which do not belong to mind. That, again, is said to be external or without the mind which is a property or quality not inhering in the mind as subject, and actually or possibly inhering in that which is a not-self or non-ego. The subjective entity in old phraseology, as of Occam and the Schoolmen, who could think precisely at least, is the real in existence,—that which has qualities special to itself,—of which it is the subject,—subject of inherence. There may be what we call material quality,—extension, figure, divisibility,—spatial quality, inhering in a non-ego which we name material, or at least do not regard as our mind, or mind at all. Or there may be mental qualities which do not inhere in me,—the individual ego,—but in another individual ego, like me, existing in time,—qualities similar to mine but numerically different. Or there may be a quality which I ascribe to the Supreme Ego—that is, a non-ego to me,—as omnipotence, omniscience, which I do not possess, which does not inhere in me, but which, as inhering in the Supreme Ego, is external to me. This is the true concept of internality and externality—the concept, to wit, of that which inheres in one subject to the exclusion of that which inheres in another, whether that be regarded as the subject of material or spiritual inherence. In this sense, externality to my consciousness is an absolute necessity, if I am to allow anything except a purely subjective or idealistic egoism. The insentient and extended are in this sense external to me. The whole space-world is so. Other selves are external; Deity is external; and to this externality it matters nothing whether, as conceived by me, those objects are always consciously conceived; — they are still conceived as externalities in the sphere of being to the internality which makes up my sphere of being. I stand in contrast to the material non-ego, as possessing specific qualities which it does not possess. I stand in contrast to other egos as possessing qualities, it may be, like theirs, yet numerically and really distinct. I stand in contrast to God, the Supreme Ego, as not possessing the qualities which He possesses, or which I attribute to Him. It is the merest self-deceptive verbalism to say that simply because I know those facts, all these things become parts of me, or depend for their reality on my knowledge, or, which comes to the same thing, on some principle—unproved and hypothetical—called Eternal or Infinite, knowing in me. This, in fact, is really to beg externality in order to destroy externality,—all the true reality of the world of being revealed in my knowledge.

Further, and this point is essential, there is no real analysis in Neo-Kantian authors of the terms which they employ. They do not use words in a definite sense—in a sense which is worthy of philosophical method. The phrases, for example, of "eternal consciousness," "infinite consciousness," are put forward absolutely without analysis, or without attempting to show what is the meaning, if any, which can by us be put into them. We have no definition, or even effort to set in definite words the meaning of those terms. Definition may be impossible and out of place, but this ought to be said, and said explicitly. People have no right to go on using words as if these had a definite sense, when they may not have this at all, and especially when the sense is not pointed out and specified.

The word "eternal" has no true application to the first principle of things until we know what that first principle is. This might be atom, or space, or time, so far as we know or can determine. "Eternal" really tells us nothing until we know what the eternal is. In Green's use there is no propriety in the word: it does not mean something enduring always; it means that which is not in time at all. This cannot possibly even be related to succession in time. Green's use of "eternal" suggests an abstraction which does not depend on this or that time, but which may be true at any time or at no time, being a mere essence thought by us—something one and indivisible—as any abstract concept is.

Then as to the term "infinite," we have the most various and conflicting applications. Usually it means simply the indefinite—that to which we can add without stop or limit, not knowing whether there is stop or limit in the thing. In numbers we can go on adding indefinitely; there is no definite number to which we cannot add, just as there is no space or time known to us which we cannot transcend. Yet this alone— this possibility of constant transcendence—tells us nothing as to the nature of the thing—whether it is completely without limits in its own being or not. Possibly this may help us to the latter conception; but the indefinite—the indefinitely increasable—never can be identified with the infinite. And the term "infinite," as that wholly without bounds, can never be applied without contradiction to an ego—a conscious ego—of which we can form any conception whatever.

The true conception of God is thus not to be found in the terms "infinite" or "eternal," or both combined. We may have these applied quite well to that which is not God, or worthy of the name. Atom may be eternal, space may be infinite; but neither would be God for us, or both combined. There might be even an eternity of duration through a whole mechanical past. We should not worship that as God.

The only approach to an adequate conception of God — the only conception which provides even for the possibility of the reality God—is that of absolute or complete independence of Causality—so far as His own being is concerned —while His action relatively to others is free. This is the conception, in a way, of our own volition. God, if at all, must rise above the line of finite regress; He cannot be a cause in that; He cannot be a cause dependent on another cause; He must be somewhere or at some point in the line of an otherwise endless scientific regress,—there above it, yet related to it, and in it,—otherwise He is nothing for us. He need not cease, being an absolute, independent cause, free and related to things, from living and constant action in all this great, varied, and wonderful world. He doubtless is the power in all,—through all—the power in whom we live, and move, and have our being. And He probably is nearer to us than those immersed in the senses and the world ever suspect, all through their happy and prosperous life; for the senses, unillumined by pure imaginative insight, or by reason, blind us to God. But whether we can fill up the concept of Him or not—whether we can point to the being who is God, or whether we must wait and follow with faltering steps His partial, ever-growing, ever-living revelation, yet we can and do know that He is and must be—seeing we know what we are, and how insufficient, dependent, and contingent is all in this experience of ours.

But do not let us suppose that we have exhausted the idea of God by "eternal," even "an eternal self-distinguishing consciousness," or by an "infinite self-consciousness," or any vague unanalysed metaphorical phrases of this sort. God is the perfect Being, the *ens realissimum*,—the Being who unites in Himself the attributes of eternity and infinity, and absolute or complete perfection. God is all that man is at his highest, —all that we can conceive of him at the best,— sublimed it may be—raised a long way above anthropomorphism, yet not merged in the impersonality of pantheism. This conception may

x

be added to in our growing knowledge and love, but can never be contradicted.

We ourselves, in the sphere of relations—in the related world—can speak of God's manifestations only in broken, diverse, incomplete phrases. Far beyond us God is, yet He is near to us in all that is—in our own selfhood, in power, in cause, in truth, goodness, and beauty—in all high ends which we can seek; He is at our door, even dimly in our hearts. But this Being can never be grasped in one conception, or treated as if He were the term or beginning of a mathematical demonstration. He is, no doubt, one and supreme. But He has endless relations,—endless, just because He is God. He is the ground of all—in all, through all,—yet somehow, not there,—not in His supreme essence, not in His selfhood, not as God. But in looking up to Him as the ground of all relations, we cannot formulate God in one conception—in one idea of the so-called reason. The only philosophy and the only religion worthy of the name is that which looks beyond pure formulæ of the mere intelligence or thought, and finds God in the breadth of experience, history, human life, yet, in Himself, utterly transcendent of all that in these we can know, feel, or name. Not the definitely Known God, not the Unknown God is our last word, far less the Unknowable God, but the ever-to-be-known God. We are not God, and when we form, or attempt to form, an idea of Him, we do not create Him. As Bossuet well said: "Si l'homme avait pu ouvertement se déclarer Dieu, son orgueil se serait emporté jusqu'à cet excès; mais se dire Dieu et se sentir mortel, l'arrogance la plus aveugle en aurait honte."

www.ingramcontent.com/pod-product-compliance
Lightning Source LLC
Chambersburg PA
CBHW021206230426
43667CB00006B/586